# QUICK WIN SOCIAL MEDIA MARKETING

## Answers to your top 100 social media marketing questions

**Annmarie Hanlon**

Published by
OAK TREE PRESS
19 Rutland Street, Cork, Ireland
www.oaktreepress.com


© 2014 Annmarie Hanlon


A catalogue record of this book is
available from the British Library.


ISBN 978 1 78119 137 8 (Paperback)
ISBN 978 1 78119 138 5 (ePub)
ISBN 978 1 78119 139 2 (Kindle)
ISBN 978 1 78119 140 8 (PDF)


Also available as an app for iPhone / iPad

# INTRODUCTION

**QUICK WIN SOCIAL MEDIA MARKETING** is aimed at busy marketing professionals with a traditional background, needing to gain a quick overview into social media for their business. It's also a useful primer for those starting their marketing journey with many practical tools, useful resources and templates that can be adapted. It contains the answers to the most frequently asked questions about social media – with sensible tips on how to adapt your business.

You can read **QUICK WIN SOCIAL MEDIA MARKETING** cover to cover, or you can dip in and out of it to find the answer to a specific question. You will find the questions and answers:

- Practical and to the point.
- Useful with constructive application for business.
- Contain valuable links to third party tools.

There are four sections to the book:

- **Social Media Marketing Essentials** sets the scene and explains how social media is used. This gives you the context, showing the move from traditional to social media marketing as well as explaining what's needed to get started.

- **Social Media Marketing Techniques** shares the elements needed to improve social media in your business. It demonstrates action you can take and share with your team.

- **Generating Sales** describes the different ways that social media can deliver sales, both free and paid-for.

- **Measuring, Monitoring & Managing** brings it all together and highlights strategic issues many managers overlook.

In addition, using the grid in the Contents, you can search for questions across a range of topics, including:

- Branding;
- Channels;
- Competition;
- Content;
- Engagement;
- Feedback;
- Mobile.

Enjoy the book! I wish you many quick wins and social media marketing success. If you have examples or case studies to share, please contact me at **annmariehanlon@evonomie.net** and I will blog about your business.

**Annmarie Hanlon**
**Birmingham**
**January 2014**

# CONTENTS

Search by theme:

Or search by topic:
Branding
Channels
Competition
Content
Engagement
Feedback
Mobile
using the grid overleaf.

## SOCIAL MEDIA MARKETING ESSENTIALS

| | Branding | Channels | Competition | Content | Engagement | Feedback | Mobile | PAGE |
|---|---|---|---|---|---|---|---|---|
| **Q17** Which social networks should I link up to? | | ☑ | | | | | | 33 |
| **Q18** What are social apps? | | ☑ | | | | | ☑ | 35 |
| **Q19** What does engagement mean in practice? | | ☑ | | | ☑ | | | 36 |
| **Q20** What content can we use online? | | | | ☑ | | | | 38 |
| **Q21** What are the principles of managing media online? | | ☑ | | ☑ | | | | 40 |
| **Q22** What is content curation? | | | | ☑ | | | | 42 |
| **Q23** What is an infographic? | | | | ☑ | | | | 43 |
| **Q24** What are personas and how do we use them? | | | | ☑ | | | | 45 |
| **Q25** How long should videos for social channels be? | | ☑ | | ☑ | | | | 47 |

## SOCIAL MEDIA MARKETING TECHNIQUES

| | Branding | Channels | Competition | Content | Engagement | Feedback | Mobile | PAGE |
|---|---|---|---|---|---|---|---|---|
| **Q26** What are the key elements of a social company page? | | ☑ | | ☑ | | | | 50 |
| **Q27** Do we need one central page or multiple local country pages? | | ☑ | | ☑ | | | | 51 |
| **Q28** How can our company page be listed in multiple industries? | | ☑ | | ☑ | | | | 52 |
| **Q29** How do I set up social company pages? | | ☑ | | ☑ | | | | 54 |

| SOCIAL MEDIA MARKETING TECHNIQUES | Branding | Channels | Competition | Content | Engagement | Feedback | Mobile | PAGE |
|---|---|---|---|---|---|---|---|---|
| **Q30** How do I manage social company pages? | | ☑ | | ☑ | | | | 56 |
| **Q31** What is SoLoMo and why does it matter? | | ☑ | | ☑ | | | ☑ | 58 |
| **Q32** What is location-based marketing? | | ☑ | | | | | ☑ | 60 |
| **Q33** What types of digital marketing campaign tools are available? | | ☑ | | ☑ | ☑ | ☑ | | 61 |
| **Q34** What are the key stages in a digital campaign? | | | | ☑ | ☑ | ☑ | | 63 |
| **Q35** How can we create a viral campaign? | | | | ☑ | ☑ | ☑ | | 64 |
| **Q36** How often should we post or update? | | | | ☑ | | | | 65 |
| **Q37** What updates can we create? | | | | ☑ | | | | 67 |
| **Q38** How do we create an infographic? | | | | ☑ | | | | 69 |
| **Q39** How do we develop personas for our business? | | | | ☑ | | | | 70 |
| **Q40** How can landing pages be used? | | | | ☑ | | | | 72 |
| **Q41** What are the critical steps in online PR? | | | | ☑ | | | | 74 |
| **Q42** What should an online press release look like? | | | | ☑ | | | | 76 |
| **Q43** What are the key issues when managing content online? | | | | ☑ | | | | 77 |
| **Q44** How do we protect our visual and written content online? | | | | ☑ | | | | 78 |
| **Q45** How do we re-use our content? | | | | ☑ | | | | 79 |

# SOCIAL MEDIA MARKETING TECHNIQUES

| | Branding | Channels | Competition | Content | Engagement | Feedback | Mobile | PAGE |
|---|---|---|---|---|---|---|---|---|
| **Q46** How do we create a simple Facebook app? | | ☑ | | ☑ | | | | 80 |
| **Q47** How do we change the order of apps on our Facebook Page? | | ☑ | | ☑ | | | | 82 |
| **Q48** Where can we demonstrate our expertise online? | ☑ | | | ☑ | | | | 83 |
| **Q49** What sales promotion activity enhances an online campaign? | | ☑ | | ☑ | ☑ | | | 84 |
| **Q50** What are the benefits of an online community? | | | | | ☑ | | | 86 |
| **Q51** How do we build a community online? | | | | | ☑ | | | 88 |
| **Q52** What tools are available to create our online community? | | | | | ☑ | | | 89 |
| **Q53** How do we build our online community? | | | | | ☑ | | | 91 |
| **Q54** How do we manage our online community? | | | | | ☑ | | | 93 |
| **Q55** How do we respond to online comments? | | | | | ☑ | ☑ | | 95 |
| **Q56** How can marketing automation make my life easier? | | | | ☑ | | | | 96 |
| **Q57** How do we see all our news feeds in one place? | | | | ☑ | | | | 97 |
| **Q58** How do we generate automatic content? | | | | ☑ | | | | 98 |
| **Q59** What tools are available to monitor our online community? | | | | | ☑ | ☑ | | 99 |
| **Q60** Why does mobile matter and what should we do? | | | | | | | ☑ | 100 |

## SOCIAL MEDIA MARKETING TECHNIQUES

| | Branding | Channels | Competition | Content | Engagement | Feedback | Mobile | PAGE |
|---|---|---|---|---|---|---|---|---|
| **Q61** Should we have a mobile app or a mobile site? | | | | | | | ☑ | 102 |
| **Q62** What are the key issues in building a mobile app? | | | | ☑ | | | ☑ | 103 |
| **Q63** What questions should we ask an agency when building a mobile app? | | | | ☑ | | | ☑ | 105 |

## GENERATING SALES

| | Branding | Channels | Competition | Content | Engagement | Feedback | Mobile | PAGE |
|---|---|---|---|---|---|---|---|---|
| **Q64** What are the key components of SEO? | | | | ☑ | | | | 108 |
| **Q65** How do we check our website for SEO? | | | | ☑ | | | | 109 |
| **Q66** How do we build SEO into our content? | | | | ☑ | | | | 110 |
| **Q67** How do we find the best keywords for our business? | | | | ☑ | | | | 111 |
| **Q68** What is pay per click (PPC) advertising? | | | | ☑ | | | | 112 |
| **Q69** What is social advertising? | | | | ☑ | ☑ | | | 114 |
| **Q70** What budget should we set for online advertising? | | | | ☑ | ☑ | | | 116 |
| **Q71** What is remarketing? | | ☑ | | | | ☑ | | 117 |
| **Q72** How do we attract followers? | | ☑ | | | | ☑ | | 118 |
| **Q73** How do we get more fans, followers and likes? | | ☑ | | | | ☑ | | 119 |

| GENERATING SALES | Branding | Channels | Competition | Content | Engagement | Feedback | Mobile | PAGE |
|---|---|---|---|---|---|---|---|---|
| **Q74** What tools can we use to acquire leads online? | | ☑ | | | ☑ | | | 121 |
| **Q75** What tools can we use to convert leads? | | ☑ | | | ☑ | | | 123 |
| **Q76** What tools can we use to retain customers? | | ☑ | | | ☑ | | | 124 |

| MEASURING, MONITORING & MANAGING | Branding | Channels | Competition | Content | Engagement | Feedback | Mobile | PAGE |
|---|---|---|---|---|---|---|---|---|
| **Q77** How do we measure a digital campaign? | | | | | | ☑ | | 128 |
| **Q78** How do we monitor a digital campaign? | | | | | | ☑ | | 129 |
| **Q79** How do we monitor brand conversations? | ☑ | | | | | ☑ | | 130 |
| **Q80** What are the key measures we should use? | | | | | | ☑ | | 131 |
| **Q81** How can we measure our social influence? | | | | | | ☑ | | 132 |
| **Q82** How do we benchmark our social marketing against competitors? | | | ☑ | | | ☑ | | 133 |
| **Q83** What tools can we use to reveal our competitors online strategies? | | | ☑ | | | | | 135 |
| **Q84** Which tools can we use to review our competitors' websites? | | | ☑ | | | | | 137 |

| MEASURING, MONITORING & MANAGING | Branding | Channels | Competition | Content | Engagement | Feedback | Mobile | PAGE |
|---|---|---|---|---|---|---|---|---|
| **Q85** How do we stop competitors commenting on our social media channels? | | | ☑ | | | | | 138 |
| **Q86** How do we monitor our competitors' activity online? | | | ☑ | | | | | 139 |
| **Q87** Where should we gain reviews for B2C? | | | | | ☑ | ☑ | | 140 |
| **Q88** Where should we gain reviews for B2B? | | | | | ☑ | ☑ | | 142 |
| **Q89** What are some easy ways to get customer feedback on our website? | | | | | ☑ | ☑ | | 143 |
| **Q90** How can we survey our customers online? | | | | | ☑ | ☑ | | 144 |
| **Q91** How can we survey non-customers online? | | | | | ☑ | ☑ | | 145 |
| **Q92** What techniques can be used to improve user experience? | | | | ☑ | ☑ | | | 146 |
| **Q93** How do we develop an online value proposition (OVP)? | | | | ☑ | ☑ | | | 148 |
| **Q94** How do we develop our editorial calendar? | | | | ☑ | | | | 150 |
| **Q95** Which management tools save time? | | | | ☑ | | | | 152 |
| **Q96** How do we add admins to our social media channels? | | ☑ | | ☑ | | | | 153 |
| **Q97** What best practice should we apply to our website and social channels? | | ☑ | | ☑ | | | | 154 |
| **Q98** How do we create a social media policy? | | ☑ | | ☑ | | | | 155 |

| MEASURING, MONITORING & MANAGING | Branding | Channels | Competition | Content | Engagement | Feedback | Mobile | PAGE |
|---|---|---|---|---|---|---|---|---|
| **Q99** Who should manage our social media? | | ☑ | | ☑ | | | | 156 |
| **Q100** How do we engage an external agency? | | | | ☑ | | | | 157 |

# SOCIAL MEDIA MARKETING ESSENTIALS

# Q1     What is social media marketing?

Social media marketing started with Facebook and LinkedIn, 10 years ago. These social networks changed the dynamics of marketing from being controlled by your company to being controlled by your customers.

The launch of the iPhone in 2007 enabled the social networks to grow dramatically as, for the first time, you didn't need a desktop computer to stay in touch. Since then, over 1 billion smartphones have been sold and we are approaching a time where everyone will be 'always connected' *via* one social network or another.

How does social media marketing impact your business? This is successful social media marketing today:

- Businesses are using Facebook to develop and launch new products;
- Charities are getting individuals to sponsor their friends *via* Twitter, Facebook and mobile;
- Professionals are endorsing their suppliers *via* LinkedIn;
- Smaller businesses are selling goods *via* Facebook and Pinterest;
- Manufacturers are using YouTube to show their expert processes;
- Hotels and venues share images of their rooms, grounds and attention to detail *via* Pinterest;

Some networks will stay the course, others will vanish and some will evolve. With over 350 social networks trying to develop their own space, competition for your content is tough. Social media marketing harnesses the power of relevant social networks to talk to your customers, generate greater insights, gain better feedback and deliver more sales for your business.

**See also**
**Q2**     What is the impact of 'social' on the marketing mix?
**Q3**     What are the key social marketing channels for B2C?
**Q4**     What are the key social marketing channels for B2B?

## Q2 What is the impact of 'social' on the marketing mix?

The traditional marketing mix is based on the 7Ps: product, price, place, promotion, physical evidence, processes and people.

The impact of social on the marketing mix is shown below. The real issue is that companies need to train staff better to respond to queries *via* social networks.

| MARKETING MIX ELEMENT | TRADITIONAL APPROACH | SOCIAL APPROACH |
|---|---|---|
| **Product** | New products are developed by a team based in the factory or office. | Fans are contacted *via* social networks to suggest, rate and test new product ideas. |
| **Price** | Prices are guarded and often not revealed until an enquiry is made or the product is seen. | Prices are transparent and easily comparable online. Your fans share how much they have paid on social networks including Facebook and TripAdvisor. |
| **Place** | Access to products is often Monday to Friday 09:00 to 17:00 for business to business (B2B) and weekends too, for business to consumer (B2C) sales. | 24/7 access to information and online shopping can take place direct from social networks. |
| **Promotion** | Print adverts are booked and planned months in advance. | Adverts can be placed on social networks within minutes to react to stock availability, positive PR and external factors. |

| MARKETING MIX ELEMENT | TRADITIONAL APPROACH | SOCIAL APPROACH |
| --- | --- | --- |
| **Physical evidence** | Packaging is functional. | Packaging contains promotional material asking the customer to share their feedback online. |
| **Processes** | The buying process often takes longer and it isn't always clear when goods will be delivered. Any complaints are managed on a one-to-one basis. | There is greater transparency in the buying process as customers can instantly 'share' information about purchases, check deliveries online and write reviews upon delivery. Similarly customers can share their complaints about delayed delivery, faulty products and poor service, with all their friends. |
| **People** | Conversations are often one-to-one; replying to a letter, discussing a matter on the telephone, or *via* an exchange of emails. | Conversations can be one-to-many. Online chat and customer feedback information can be shared easily on social networks and read by friends of your fans. |

**See also**

Q1    What is social media marketing?
Q3    What are the key social marketing channels for B2C?
Q4    What are the key social marketing channels for B2B?
Q10   How do we adapt our traditional brand for online marketing?
Q49   What sales promotion activity enhances an online campaign?
Q69   What is social advertising?
Q98   How do we create a social media policy?

## Q3      What are the key social marketing channels for B2C?

The table below prioritises the current key social channels for business to consumer. If you have limited time, focus on the channel that includes your target customers.

| CHANNEL | WHAT'S IT ABOUT? | WHO USES IT? | B2C USE? |
| --- | --- | --- | --- |
| **Facebook** | Facebook pages have been created by household brands, public figures and small businesses. | Used by 1 billion+ people across the USA & Europe. Becoming popular with older users for keeping tabs on children and grandchildren. | To stay in touch with customers, recruit new customers, promote offers and advertise to a highly targeted market. |
| **Instagram** | A fun way to share photos from your mobile phone and add effects. Owned by Facebook and popular with designer brands, journalists and photographers. A photo taken with a mobile phone has been changed *via* instagram and used as a cover photo for the New York Times. | Popular with women and has a younger audience. | Useful if you have 'behind the scenes' photography or wish to showcase a process that wouldn't be seen on a formal website. |

| CHANNEL | WHAT'S IT ABOUT? | WHO USES IT? | B2C USE? |
|---------|------------------|--------------|----------|
| **Pinterest** | A visual medium to showcase products *via* pictures and videos, used by household and designer brands. | Mainly 'women with wallets' and time. Popular with people organising special events such as weddings and parties. | To build your brand and reach out to new social audiences. To drive traffic to your website, especially product pages. |
| **Twitter** | This short message service has added images and short video. | A mix of users (including journalists, politicians and public figures) have a Twitter address, so it's popular with people seeking news. | To stay in touch with customers, promote offers and engage target customers. Advertising options drive traffic to your website. |
| **YouTube** | YouTube is the second largest search engine in Europe. | Approaching 1 billion monthly users, many ages. | Useful for product launches, sharing TV adverts, raising brand awareness. Videos don't need to be super-slick, home-made versions can work successfully. Great way to show answers to FAQs and get your customer-facing team closer to customers. |

All these channels can be integrated – for example, your latest YouTube video can be shared on Facebook and Twitter and as an image pinned to Pinterest.

**See also**

# Q4 What are the key social marketing channels for B2B?

The business-to-business environment is more formal. The current key social networks require a degree of etiquette, good spelling, responding to enquiries and a business rather than personal approach. You need to consider carefully which networks to use.

| CHANNEL | WHAT'S IT ABOUT? | WHO USES IT? | B2B USE? |
|---|---|---|---|
| Blogs | Content is a key element of marketing. All social channels seek content whether it's words, images or video. | People searching for information: Blogs are often found *via* search engines or because their information is linked on another social channel. | Blogs are a great way to share content. Add tags and keywords into your content and links back to your own website for search engine optimisation (SEO) purposes. When integrated into your website, this is a useful tool to keep your website up-to-date. |
| Facebook | Used by household brands, public figures and small businesses. | It's harder for B2B to engage with customers on Facebook – but claim your brand name and update occasionally. | Mainly seen as a recruitment channel for B2B. |

| CHANNEL | WHAT'S IT ABOUT? | WHO USES IT? | B2B USE? |
|---|---|---|---|
| **Google+** | Google+ is owned by the most popular search engine worldwide. It is a blend of Facebook and LinkedIn. | A fast-growing user base, more popular with a 'techie' audience and men. | To add events, to add links to your blog and to connect with others. It also has a useful business function 'Google Hangouts', enabling you to create a hangout and share computer screens, ideal for online customer services and training. |
| **LinkedIn** | Developing business applications, including sales packages that enable teams to identify and contact potential customers and recruitment packages that deliver references. | 200 million professionals, mainly in Europe and the USA, use LinkedIn to stay in touch, track their contacts and share key information. | Use the basic membership to keep track of where key contacts are and identify who they know. Pay a premium subscription to use as a sales tool to find prospects, build leads and contact potential customers. |

| CHANNEL | WHAT'S IT ABOUT? | WHO USES IT? | B2B USE? |
|---|---|---|---|
| Slideshare | Owned by LinkedIn, it is a way of sharing slide presentations and PDFs. Its main benefit is the search engine optimisation (SEO) value of driving traffic from a well-regarded website to your website. | Businesses, students and educators seeking knowledge. | Add tags and keywords into your presentations and links back to your own website for SEO purposes. Showcase your skills and work done: it's a little like Pinterest for business. |
| Twitter | This short message service has added images and short video. | A mix of users (including journalists, politicians and public figures) have a Twitter address, so it's popular with people seeking news. | To stay in touch with customers, promote offers and engage target customers. Advertising options drive traffic to your website. |
| YouTube | YouTube is the second largest search engine in Europe. | Not specifically used by business users, but a good way to send customers videos or testimonials to demonstrate work done. | A gift for manufacturers to demonstrate how your product is made or can be used. Useful way to answer FAQs using a video medium. |

**See also**

# Q5   Should our business use group buying channels?

Group buying started in 1977 when the Home Shopping Network was founded after 112 electric can openers were sold on a Florida radio station programme.

A group buying channel can be useful if your business:

- Wants to move excess or old stock;
- Needs to reach new audiences, such as students seeking an offer on a Monday;
- Is a venue such as a hotel or spa and wants to fill 'quiet times';

Group buying is fraught with challenges and has created difficulties for numerous small businesses. These include the cupcake bakery Need a Cake, which offered a 75% discount on 12 cupcakes, which normally cost $30, and underestimated the response, resulting in an extra 8,500 customers and a €15,000 loss, or Posies Café, which lost nearly $8,000 with its Groupon campaign and had to use personal savings to cover payroll and rent.

You should only use group buying if you:

- Have the time to manage the process;
- Can get your staff to support the deal;
- Don't need instant cashflow as you often have to wait for some weeks or until the deal is completely finished (which could take some months) before you get your income;
- Are good at negotiating with commission-based sales people who work for the group buying companies.

Critical factors that affect group buying are:

- **Customer retention:** Group buying customers often are deal-hunters, so they go from place to place depending on a deal, and are not always seeking a long-term solution;

- **Local access:** The offer must be locally-based to achieve conversion rates – for example, 'Dublin spa offers 2 for 1 on Monday';

- **Consumer trust:** People are naturally suspicious if an offer looks too good to be true. Be specific about your terms and conditions and ensure the customer has read these before they pay.

To explore group buying further, look at **www.groupon.co.uk**, **www.livingsocial.com** and **www.wowcher.co.uk** to explore which of your competitors have signed up to sell offers in this way.

**See also**
Q3      What are the key social marketing channels for B2C?
Q4      What are the key social marketing channels for B2B?
Q6      How does group buying work?
Q76     What tools can we use to retain customers?

## Q6    How does group buying work?

There are two aspects to group buying. The first is the group buying company; the second is your business.

The group buying company needs a range of staff in different roles:

- Sales staff to negotiate, close and manage the deal with the supplier (you);
- Editorial staff to create offer descriptions to drive consumer interest;
- IT staff to create and manage systems;
- Marketing staff to promote and manage the brand;
- Management teams to manage the process, product offers, pricing strategies;
- Finance staff for managing cashflow.

Typically, the sales staff telephone you, make an appointment and get you to agree to a deal quickly.

In your business, you need staff to:

- Agree which products or services will be nominated (such as old stock, slow selling items, quiet days);
- Decide how these will be managed (for three months' only, every Monday);
- Identify software solutions to manage the bookings – you don't want to block your standard telephone number, which will upset your existing customers;
- Agree who will manage the bookings and how you will up-sell or re-sell to these customers;
- Agree how the process will work – for example, if a regular customer has paid €50 for a haircut and an offer customer has paid €20, do you want them sitting next to each other with the offer customer telling everyone about their deal?

The critical factors to managing group buying are:

- Set limits: numbers of offers, days of the week the offer is valid, expiry dates, maximum numbers that can be redeemed and the offer time period;

- Get staff involved early so they are involved and motivated;

- Work out what is – and isn't – included;

- Clearly note all conditions;

- Consider the buying process – ideally, your offer customers should place the order online; if this isn't possible, consider a separate campaign telephone number;

- Cashflow: Do you have sufficient cashflow to finance the production of the extra orders, additional staff needed and management of the coupons? If not, avoid group offer deals!

**See also**

Q5    Should our business use group buying channels?

# Q7 Where do I source ideas online for a new business or product?

"Necessity is the mother of all invention" and traditionally new product ideas are generated from a need: yours or your customers'.

Social media marketing enables businesses to 'crowdsource': to go to groups of people online and source ideas from them. Sources for new ideas can come from:

- **Facebook:** Used by Walkers Crisps, Marmite food spread and Vitamin Water for new flavours and products;

- **Your blog or forum:** RS Components generates new ideas *via* its engineers' forum;

- Groups such as LinkedIn groups, where the members seek advice from others;

- Social networks like Quora (**www.quora.com**) where you can post questions.

- Online platforms where you pay a fee for the ideas, for example: **www.ideascale.com**, **www.innocentive.com**, **www.hypios.com** and **www.wazoku.com**.

The online platforms post and circulate your idea request to a worldwide audience, giving you the opportunity to poll thousands of creative people. It is a much cheaper route to getting an idea than setting up a R&D team. To make it work, you need to ensure that you have prepared a clear brief that states exactly what you need, who for and why.

**See also**
Q8   How can I test new ideas online?
Q90  How can we survey our customers online?
Q91  How can we survey non-customers online?

## Q8      How can I test new ideas online?

Computer games makers often create 100 or more games to generate one winning idea. One way to narrow down the initial development of your product or business idea is to test it online. This can be achieved:

- By surveying your existing customers using a platform like **www.surveymonkey.com** or **www.polldaddy.com**.

- By surveying your target customers through a third party such as LinkedIn (contact **surveys@linkedin.com**) or **www.google.com/insights/consumersurveys**.

- Use an online platform like **www.quirky.com**, **www.usurv.com** or **www.spigit.com**.

If you have a great idea, friends and family often will agree with you – even though they have no experience in the area or have reservations (they don't want to upset you). Testing online gives your idea a better chance of success with feedback from a wider group that may have more experience in your area. Many large companies use these services when refining new concepts.

To avoid the challenge of sharing your idea online where it could be seen by your competitors, some websites enable you to keep the idea 'private' – although this usually involves an additional fee.

**See also**
Q7      Where do I source ideas online for a new business or product?
Q90     How can we survey our customers online?
Q91     How can we survey non-customers online?

# Q9 What images do I need for social channels?

All the social channels require a cover page and logo.

The cover page for Facebook, Google+ and Twitter changes from time to time. What is a nuisance for all businesses is that there is no standard format size for these cover pages; they are all slightly different. It's wise therefore to get some standard designs prepared and adapted to use in your different social channels.

| CHANNEL | LOCATION | SIZE | NOTE |
|---------|----------|------|------|
| Facebook | Company page cover | 851 x 315 pixels. | The logo space is 24 pixels from the left-hand side. Leave some clear space near your logo. |
| Facebook | Logo space | 180 x 180 pixels. | Shows as 160 x 160, include bleed space around edges. |
| Google + | Pages cover photo | 960 x 540 pixels; minimum 480 x 270 pixels, maximum 2120 x 1192 pixels. | The logo (profile photo) is added in the centre. This means that any text you may wish to add (such as your web address) could be at the top. |
| LinkedIn | Company page cover | 646 x 220 pixels. | Your logo is added by LinkedIn and is not near the banner! |
| Pinterest | Logo space | 160 × 165 pixels. | Square logo only. Add bleed space as logo is cropped. |

| CHANNEL | LOCATION | SIZE | NOTE |
|---------|----------|------|------|
| **Twitter** | Design header | 1200 x 600 pixels. | If you have a long name and have used your full bio space, there is not much room for more. You'll need to use the corners of the design header.<br>Your profile image or logo is added by Twitter. |
| **YouTube** | Branded Channel central area | 1280 × 350 pixels. | YouTube has several areas for logo and not all are visible. In addition, the top left and bottom right areas may be hidden by the profile image (avatar) and social media icons. |

Cover pages should change with the seasons and are designed to reflect what's happening in your business at that moment in time. The logo is the one constant. The best approach is to ask a designer to create five or six cover pages for the whole year, which can be adapted for each of the social networks you use. This means you are constantly ready to refresh your cover pages and stay ahead. It's also cheaper to work with a designer on several cover pages at the same time, rather than making several appointments over the year.

**See also**
Q3      What are the key social marketing channels for B2C?
Q4      What are the key social marketing channels for B2B?
Q13     How do we source images online?
Q14     How do we protect our brand assets?

## Q10 How do we adapt our traditional brand for online marketing?

Traditional brands often exist in an environment where brochures are posted to customers, products are ordered *via* telephone or fax and questions to staff normally are received *via* letter. Online marketing moves the whole business into a public and social space that moves faster and thus usually requires significant changes in the way the business works.

To adapt your business, look at the following elements and see what you can change (what you need to change) and how.

| ELEMENT | CHANGES NEEDED |
|---|---|
| Brand Identity | Adapt your company's logo to fit into social media spaces, which may mean changing it from a rectangular shape to a square or round shape. Capture your brand online: for example, claim your Facebook page, Twitter name. |
| Product | Identify whether any of your products or services can be sold online. Perhaps you can offer training *via* webinars (online seminars). If not, can you showcase your products online? |
| Price | Can you show your prices online? Can you explain how your pricing works? |
| Promotion | Online promotion has made advertising more accessible for smaller businesses. Would your business benefit from targeted online adverts? |
| Physical Evidence | Can your printed materials be converted into electronic documents or presentations? |
| Processes | Are there ways to improve your sales or customer processes online? For example, to place orders online, to check stock levels, to access drawings or reports? |

| ELEMENT | CHANGES NEEDED |
|---------|----------------|
| People | Respond to customer comments and feedback promptly, recognising that you do so in a public environment. Can you prepare standard phrases to be used to address the questions you receive most frequently? |

Some of your competitors may have adapted their businesses. Why not explore how they achieved this online to see what is and isn't possible?

**See also**

Q1      What is social media marketing?

Q2      What is the impact of 'social' on the marketing mix?

Q11     How do we assess our digital strengths and weaknesses?

Q12     How do we ensure our brand is consistent online?

Q14     How do we protect our brand assets?

Q21     What are the principles of managing media online?

Q77     How do we measure a digital campaign?

Q78     How do we monitor a digital campaign?

Q97     What best practice should we apply to our website and social channels?

Q98     How do we create a social media policy?

# Q11   How do we assess our digital strengths and weaknesses?

Strengths and weaknesses are within a company's control. Your digital strengths and weaknesses indicate where you need more help or have work to do. Use the template below to assess your business.

| QUESTION | WHAT THIS MEANS | YES / NO | WORK TO DO |
|---|---|---|---|
| **Does your business have one person in overall control of digital?** | If the website is managed by marketing, the Facebook page looked after by PR and LinkedIn by someone else, it can lead to different messages in different places and lack of integration. | | |
| **Has your business captured its brand name(s) in relevant social channels?** | Not yet signed up for Twitter? Still thinking about Google+? It's wise to secure all the social networks with your brand name as if you wait, another business with the same name in another country might get there first. | | |
| **Has your business completed all its online profiles?** | When you have secured the social channels, it's a good idea to upload your logo and add some information about your business on each, directing all the traffic back to your website. | | |
| **Does your business use customers to generate prospect leads online?** | Happy customers will provide recommendations, add reviews and tell others about you. What are you doing to maximise these opportunities? | | |

| QUESTION | WHAT THIS MEANS | YES / NO | WORK TO DO |
|---|---|---|---|
| **Does your business listen in and join in with customers' conversations online?** | Your customers might be talking about you online! Use Google Alerts to see who's talking about you and where. | | |
| **Does your business respond to customers online?** | Respond to all comments – good and bad. Potential customers read the management responses as well as customers' comments. | | |
| **Has your business linked its social channels back to its corporate website?** | Your website is the only channel you own and control. The social spaces can change so it's essential to drive traffic back to your own website. | | |
| **Who owns the social databases?** | If your staff make contact on LinkedIn with customers, during work time, are they your contacts, theirs or is this unclear? Make sure it's understood by all. | | |

**See also**

## Q12 How do we ensure our brand is consistent online?

The challenge with digital marketing is the different requirements for your brand's appearance and style in so many places. Twitter wants a square logo, Facebook wants the same but with added space and Google+ will place your logo into a circle. This all means your brand could look inconsistent online.

To ensure brand consistency, you should:

- Work with your graphic designer to create different logo formats for the different social networks.

- Prepare imagery that can be used in all the social networks and clearly identifies the business, regardless of where the customer is looking.

- Create a 'boilerplate' – that is, a key statement about your business that adapts to both a short and a long sentence.

- Agree the name style. Is your business 'ABC Limited', 'A.B.C. Limited' or 'ABC Ltd'? When you've agreed the name, ensure this is shared with staff so they use the same format too all the time. The style should reflect your website domain name as this will be needed when you register your company name in LinkedIn and Facebook, as well as on other future social networks.

**See also**
**Q10**   How do we adapt our traditional brand for online marketing?
**Q14**   How do we protect our brand assets?
**Q15**   How do we protect our reputation online?
**Q79**   How do we monitor brand conversations?

## Q13    How do we source images online?

Many social networks are moving towards greater use of images. For B2B service organisations, this can be a challenge! Creating fantastic images of your staff delivering great service is not always easy.

You can source images from a wide range of online sources, including:

- **www.dreamstime.com**
- **www.fotolia.com**
- **www.freeirishphotos.com**
- **www.gettyimages.com**
- **www.stockfreeimages.com**

Beware! When you find images online and want to use them for your own website, you either need to pay for them and/or credit the source.

If it's a professional photo stock selling website, you will need to state how you will use the image (online, offline) and agree the resolution needed in order to finalise the price of the image. This is a much cheaper option than taking an image from one of these sites and removing their logo as these companies will find out, send you a letter from their legal team and bill you for unauthorised use of their images. And it can be costly! The average penalty is €700, so it's cheaper to pay up-front.

**See also**
**Q9**    What images do I need for social channels?
**Q14**   How do we protect our brand assets?
**Q38**   How do we create an infographic?
**Q44**   How do we protect our visual and written content online?

## Q14    How do we protect our brand assets?

Your brand assets include your:

- Company name.
- Written content.
- Images.
- Videos.
- Podcasts or other recordings.

You can either share or sell your brand assets. Sharing is a key factor in social marketing. To protect your brand assets when you share:

- Build in hyperlinks back to your website.
- Add your logo where relevant.
- Include your web address in a space where it doesn't detract from the content.
- State your rules on your intellectual property – for example: 'Please feel free to share, but do credit ABC company'. In the example below, Julia's Creations encourages users to share her images and explains the rules.

---

**About**

http://juliasgreetings.blogspot.co.uk/
Feel free to tag & 'share' my pictures, but please give proper credit if you re-post my pictures. All picture posts by © Julia's Creations are copyright protected & cannot be altered in anyway.

---

If your business is a limited company, you might want to consider protecting your intellectual property in the company name itself by obtaining a trade mark *via* the Patent or Trade Mark Office. A trade mark gives you greater control of where, when and how your company name is used. Otherwise, success may lead to genericisation – when people talk now of 'hoovering', most don't realise that 'Hoover' is the brand name of a specific make of vacuum cleaner but its uniqueness has been lost as the name has fallen into general use to refer to ALL vacuum cleaners. Google is another example of a brand name that has become genericised – we talk of 'Googling' something, when we really mean 'search online using the Google search engine'.

**See also**
**Q10**     How do we adapt our traditional brand for online marketing?
**Q12**     How do we ensure our brand is consistent online?
**Q15**     How do we protect our reputation online?
**Q79**     How do we monitor brand conversations?

# Q15    How do we protect our reputation online?

Your reputation can make or break your business and, in a social environment, the wrong message can spread quickly and it can be expensive to find a remedy. Protecting your reputation online involves three steps:

- Setting up an alert service to monitor mentions of your company or brand(s).
- Reading these mentions.
- Responding the right way.

### Setting up an alert service to monitor mentions

Google Alerts is a free tool that notifies you when your search terms are mentioned. The search terms can include your name, company name and product brand names. There is no limit on the number of alerts you can create.

### Reading the mentions

It's not enough to be notified, you need to read the mentions, reviews and comments. For businesses, this can include reviews on different types of websites:

- **Business-based:** LinkedIn, Quora.
- **Location-based:** Foursquare, Facebook places.
- **Search-based:** Google+.
- **Hospitality and leisure:** TripAdvisor® and booking sites.

### Responding the right way

For location- and search-based websites, your company should claim its space. This is straightforward and means going to the relevant website and clicking on 'claim as owner' or 'is this your business?'. Usually once you have registered your details, you must wait for a code to be sent *via* post to verify your ownership. Once you've staked your claim, you are able to respond.

It's important to:

- Respond to all reviews – both good and bad.
- Don't forget the first line is the most visible, so use this to *positively* promote your business.
- Don't argue with a customer. If something has gone wrong, start with something positive – 'thank you so much for taking the time to share your feedback' – and apologise if something did go wrong – 'I am personally really sorry that this happened. It would be great to have a chat about this and I wonder if you're able to contact me (give your email address) so I can ensure this doesn't happen again'.

**See also**
Q12   How do we ensure our brand is consistent online?
Q14   How do we protect our brand assets?
Q16   What legal issues can impact my business online?
Q79   How do we monitor brand conversations?
Q97   What best practice should we apply to our website and social channels?

# Q16 What legal issues can impact my business online?

There are over 300 laws across Europe that have an impact on marketing, depending on your business category. Legal issues that can affect your business online include:

- Staff making defamatory comments about others.
- Celebrity bloggers being paid to promote your products/services, but not disclosing this (misleading practices).
- Stealing images from other websites (copyright infringement).
- Using well-known brand names on your own website (passing off).
- Paying for brand names *via* AdWords (passing off).

These issues (and more) should be covered in your terms and conditions of employment or company handbook. You may not want to state explicitly that staff 'cannot say negative things about the company on Facebook' (you'd have to list every social channel, since an exception might imply permission!) but you should say that staff 'should not bring the company into disrepute.' Check your terms and conditions and ensure all staff are aware of potential consequences online.

Best practice with customers is to:

- Gain *consent* as the law doesn't mention 'opt-in'. Ensure you record when and from whom the consent was obtained.
- Have a legally compliant website with information on cookies and your full contact details.
- Ensure your privacy policy is easy to find and understand.
- Stick to data protection guidelines and adopt the law everywhere.

**See also**
**Q12**   How do we ensure our brand is consistent online?
**Q14**   How do we protect our brand assets?
**Q15**   How do we protect our reputation online?
**Q79**   How do we monitor brand conversations?

**Q97**   What best practice should we apply to our website and social
channels?

## Q17 Which social networks should I link up to?

Some networks are more social than others! On Twitter, many tweets a day are acceptable, while LinkedIn users may see others as 'noisy' if they share excessively. In fact, LinkedIn removed the function to add a Twitter feed to LinkedIn updates for this reason.

If your business sells to consumers, your main platform is Facebook and it's OK to connect all relevant social networks, such as those shown below. This means when you add an image to Pinterest or Instagram, it will appear on Facebook and *vice versa*. This is useful, as it adds content to all your networks.

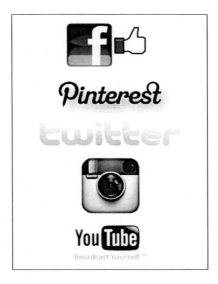

If your business sells to other businesses, your main platform is LinkedIn, so you should connect to other networks with caution. LinkedIn has a more professional tone and you don't want to overdo your posts. But do connect *from* LinkedIn to other networks such as Twitter and don't forget that your LinkedIn posts can include presentations added to your profile.

**See also**

**Q3**      What are the key social marketing channels for B2C?
**Q4**      What are the key social marketing channels for B2B?
**Q77**    How do we measure a digital campaign?
**Q78**    How do we monitor a digital campaign?
**Q98**    How do we create a social media policy?

# Q18    What are social apps?

Applications, better known as apps, enable users to perform a task. The task could be to post on your company page, upload content into your social networks or connect to others.

There are many types of social apps – for example:

| APP TYPE | EXAMPLES |
|---|---|
| Calculate / Utility | Supermarket apps, Calculators |
| Shopping | Amazon, eBay, BuyandSell.ie |
| Games | Angry Birds, Candy Crush |
| References | Wikipedia, Daft.ie |
| Entertainment | Spotify, Kindle |
| News | Sky, CNN |
| Productivity | Bookmarks, Documents, Web Standard Colours |
| Search Tool | Google, Bing |
| Social Networking | Facebook, Twitter, Instagram |
| Sports | GolfGPS, Irish Trails |
| Travel | Trip Advisor, Hailo, Passport Minder, mustDART |
| Weather | World Weather, iWeather |

There are also apps within social media sites, such as the standard apps in Facebook or those that events and apps companies create, which may include 'sign up here', games and other applications designed to capture customer data.

**See also**
Q46    How do we create a simple Facebook app?
Q61    Should we have a mobile app or a mobile site?
Q62    What are the key issues in building a mobile app?
Q63    What questions should we ask an agency when building a mobile app?

## Q19    What does engagement mean in practice?

Creating content is the first step in engagement, but the real issue is getting the customer to respond – or to engage. This means creating material that encourages customers to take action, which may include:

- Sharing your content with their friends who may be potential customers.
- Commenting on your content which indirectly shares this with friends.
- Liking.
- Forwarding to a friend.
- Signing up for information.
- Taking some other action.

Engagement with your customers depends on your social marketing goals. These may be to:

- Differentiate your business from the competition.
- Remind customers that you exist.
- Inform customers and potential customers of your services.
- Persuade potential customers to do business with you.
- Drive traffic to your website.
- Reach new audiences that would not traditionally contact you.
- Generate leads.
- Convert leads.
- Generate sales.
- Engage customers.
- Retain customers.
- Create advocates.

Start by deciding your goals and understanding what's relevant for your customers.

**See also**

## Q20    What content can we use online?

It is better to create your own content rather than to use material from other websites, because unique content provides information or an experience that users cannot get elsewhere. But creating your own content means advance planning to organise graphics, words and movies. Think about existing materials within your business and how they can be re-purposed.

Online content formats include:

- Slide presentations.
- PDFs.
- Videos with, and without, voice.
- Short comments.
- Longer updates.
- White papers.
- Images.
- Podcasts (voice recordings).

Content format is one issue, the other is the type of content. This can be:

- Free downloads.
- Useful documents.
- Helpful or funny images.
- Infographics.
- Checklists.

Start by looking at your competitors' websites and see what content they use and how.

**See also**
Q9      What images do I need for social channels?
Q13     How do we source images online?
Q21     What are the principles of managing media online?
Q22     What is content curation?

**Q23** What is an infographic?
**Q37** What updates can we create?
**Q38** How do we create an infographic?
**Q43** What are the key issues when managing content online?
**Q44** How do we protect our visual and written content online?
**Q45** How do we re-use our content?
**Q58** How do we generate automatic content?
**Q66** How do we build SEO into our content?
**Q94** How do we develop our editorial calendar?

## Q21　What are the principles of managing media online?

The three principles of managing media online and your digital assets are:

- Protect.
- Distribute.
- Maximise.

### Protect your digital assets

Ensure the images you use belong to your business, contain your identification (web address, logo, company name) and focus on your key business messages.

### Distribute your digital assets

Create content worth sharing! For example:

- Numbers, facts, figures.
- Make it easy to share.
- Optimise for sharing: resize, different formats.
- Always add an image.
- Identify advocates and share with them.

### Maximise your digital assets

Start with a piece of content – for example, conduct a survey and then:

- Write a white paper about the findings – add this to your website, or make it downloadable from your blog.
- Create a summary in PowerPoint – add this to Slideshare and social bookmarking sites.
- Graphically illustrate key points as an infographic – add it to Pinterest, Facebook.
- Film one of the team talking about the key points from the survey – add the video to Pinterest or YouTube.

- Share links to the above over time on all social networks.

**See also**

Q12    How do we ensure our brand is consistent online?
Q14    How do we protect our brand assets?
Q15    How do we protect our reputation online?
Q20    What content can we use online?
Q43    What are the key issues when managing content online?
Q44    How do we protect our visual and written content online?
Q77    How do we measure a digital campaign?
Q78    How do we monitor a digital campaign?
Q97    What best practice should we apply to our website and social channels?
Q98    How do we create a social media policy?

# Q22　What is content curation?

According to marketing guru Seth Godin, content marketing is the only marketing left!

Creating content is the single greatest challenge in social marketing. Original, well-considered content takes time to research, write and edit.

The alternative is to curate or borrow content from others. For example, if your business creates software, you could review different articles about selecting software and link them back to your business. It's important to always credit the original content source or the writer may come back with an accusation of plagiarism at best – a law suit at worst!

Curating content takes less time and can enable your post to get to a wider audience, especially if you are name-dropping. People being mentioned often like to share content that includes their name or photo!

Websites like Mashable.com often include curated content, for example articles like:

- 15 digital resources you may have missed.
- 10 apps for the great outdoors.
- 5 websites for start-up businesses.

**See also**

## Q23    What is an infographic?

An infographic is a piece of information turned into a graphic. Instead of reading a long list of data, many companies have started to make key facts and figures easier to understand by adopting an image-led approach.

Sage Ireland created the infographic below about doing business in Ireland. Note that it includes their logo, is created in Sage's corporate colour and the company's social networks are mentioned. Most important, the actual content is interesting which makes it more likely to be shared across a wider audience.

Look at **www.informationisbeautiful.net** to see how infographics can turn into art!

**See also**
**Q20**    What content can we use online?
**Q38**    How do we create an infographic?

## Q24    What are personas and how do we use them?

A persona is an imaginary person. The idea is to create 'personas' that closely match your key customers as a more focused approach to sales: rather than 'one size fits all' or 'we sell to anybody', using a persona enables your business to tailor its offers to specific customer categories. This saves time and money on marketing since you aim at the right people.

For example, Astronomy Ireland, a popular astronomy club, has members who range from those with a professional interest to those who enjoy looking at the stars for fun. Members' levels of education vary from PhDs in astronomy to those with little formal education, so from this information we can create a matrix and identify the different personas.

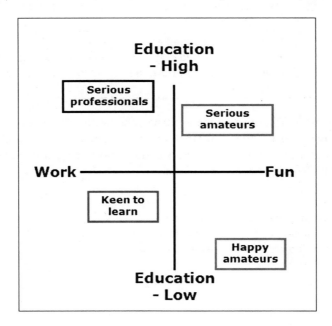

Astronomy Ireland has given names to each of these different groups of customers. To create personas, we need to add more detail, based on which we can determine the appropriate marketing action – for example:

| PERSONA | DETAIL | MARKETING ACTION |
|---|---|---|
| **Serious professionals** | Aged 35 to 65, Dublin-based, interested in conferences, scientific reports. | Send conference information, invites to sign up for scientific reports. |
| **Serious amateurs** | Aged 40 to 55, based within 50 kilometres of Dublin, interested in gaining formal qualifications and conferences. | Send training programmes, conference information, invites to sign up for scientific reports. |
| **Keen to learn** | Aged 45 to 60, based across Ireland, interested in Saturday and evening workshops, newsletters. | Send workshop information, invites to sign up for newsletters. |
| **Happy amateurs** | Aged 45 to 75, based across Ireland, interested in evening workshops, newsletters, the club. | Send workshop information, invites to sign up for club membership. |

The more you can develop the personas, the better. Try to give each an actual name, even add a photograph (for internal use only!). Use the personas when testing new marketing ideas, developing your website or considering new products or services.

**See also**
Q20    What content can we use online?
Q21    What are the principles of managing media online?
Q39    How do we develop personas for our business?

## Q25 How long should videos for social channels be?

Since YouTube has over 1 billion unique users and over 4 billion hours of video are watched on it each month, it can be a challenge to get your video seen! In pre-Internet times, businesses would commission corporate videos that ran for at least 10 minutes, if not 20. These days the most-viewed videos are short – according to Unruly Media, the average video length for the top 50 most-shared global video ads is just over four minutes. The top 10 average 4 minutes 11 seconds (2,513 total seconds – excluding "Kony 2012"), while the next 10 average 2 minutes 30 seconds (1,501 total seconds).

If you're creating a business-related video for social channels, it's essential that it should:

- Get the viewer's attention from the start.
- Communicate the point succinctly.
- Focus on one issue.
- Include a call to action.
- Include your keywords.

Don't worry about whether your video is *exactly* 30, 60 or 90 seconds, its playing time can vary with digital devices and doesn't need to be a specific length. Shorter can be sweeter as Twitter has bought Vine, a mini video clip application that allows you to take a video with your mobile phone and upload it to Twitter. Vine videos are only six seconds long!

**See also**
**Q21** What are the principles of managing media online?

# SOCIAL MEDIA MARKETING TECHNIQUES

## Q26    What are the key elements of a social company page?

Company pages are available in many social networks. The most popular are Facebook, LinkedIn and Google+. All company pages need the same key elements:

| ELEMENT | EXPLANATION |
| --- | --- |
| Company logo | The logo size changes depending on the social network. |
| Banner | Also known as the cover page, the banner is a place for your business to visually highlight its products or services, adapted to the requirements of each social network. |
| Company information | A short sentence that includes your keywords and web address. |
| Photos | Images your business owns or has paid to use in this space. |
| Products and services | Descriptions of your products and services, including keywords and images. |
| Videos | Some company pages include the option to add videos. |

It's wise to prepare your materials in a Word document, and then to copy and paste the text into the different pages. This ensures the spelling is correct and that all pages are consistent. It also means you have a base copy to work from when the next new social network comes along!

**See also**
Q3    What are the key social marketing channels for B2C?
Q4    What are the key social marketing channels for B2B?
Q10    How do we adapt our traditional brand for online marketing?
Q12    How do we ensure our brand is consistent online?
Q27    Do we need one central page or multiple local country pages?
Q28    How can our company page be listed in multiple industries?
Q29    How do I set up social company pages?
Q30    How do I manage social company pages?

# Q27 Do we need one central page or multiple local country pages?

Some businesses operate in many locations and need to decide whether to create one central/global page or multiple pages for different countries.

There are advantages and disadvantages with both options. How you decide depends on the skills and resources inside your business.

| OPTIONS | ADVANTAGES | DISADVANTAGES |
|---|---|---|
| One company page | Easy to maintain. Can build larger fan base. One global audience. | If in one language, this may not meet the needs of all your customers. Engagement may be reduced as customers don't identify with the content on page. |
| Multiple company pages | Focused communications to specific customer groups. Can deliver more 'authentic' content. | Requires more admin support. Customers may 'like' the wrong page. |

**See also**
Q26   What are the key elements of a social company page?
Q28   How can our company page be listed in multiple industries?
Q29   How do I set up social company pages?
Q30   How do I manage social company pages?

## Q28    How can our company page be listed in multiple industries?

Some businesses sell different products to different groups of customers and understandably want to show different pages to those different groups. The table below shows where and how this is possible.

| SOCIAL CHANNEL | MULTIPLE PAGES – YES OR NO? | NOTE |
| --- | --- | --- |
| **Facebook** | Simply create the page and name it CompanyCountry to distinguish from other pages. | Facebook now permits 'Verified Pages' so brand names or well-known companies can claim their own names. |
| **Instagram** | The same as Twitter, you can set up separate Instagram accounts but will need separate email addresses for each. | If creating different accounts decide on which Facebook and Twitter accounts you wish to share the images. |
| **LinkedIn** | More challenging as LinkedIn recognises a company based on the email addresses. So if your company email address is a .com for all locations, only one page is permitted. | LinkedIn allows you to target updates based on audience groups, so company page news can be shared to specific locations only. |
| **Pinterest** | Similar to LinkedIn in its approach, Pinterest enables business accounts to be set up *via* a verified domain, so if your company has a .com for the whole business, you can only set up one verified account. | You may need technical assistance from your web team to verify your account as some code has to be placed on your website. |

| SOCIAL CHANNEL | MULTIPLE PAGES – YES OR NO? | NOTE |
|---|---|---|
| **Twitter** | You can set up separate Twitter accounts but will need separate email addresses for each. So if like Dell, you want seven or eight Twitter accounts, you'll need to use different company email addresses. | Don't forget if a member of staff leaves and you've used their email address for the Twitter account, you'll need to maintain that email address or change it on Twitter. |
| **YouTube** | You can set up separate YouTube channels (accounts) but will need to set up separate Google accounts and email addresses for each. | Managing multiple Google accounts can be challenging! Consider whether you need separate accounts or could add all content to one YouTube account. |

**See also**

Q26    What are the key elements of a social company page?
Q27    Do we need one central page or multiple local country pages?
Q29    How do I set up social company pages?
Q30    How do I manage social company pages?

## Q29     How do I set up social company pages?

Setting up pages is fairly straightforward. It requires some time, attention to detail and consistent use of the same information. To prepare your information, see **Q26** and follow the instructions below.

| SOCIAL CHANNEL | INSTRUCTIONS |
|---|---|
| **Facebook** | Go to **www.facebook.com/pages/create/** and follow the on-screen instructions. |
| **Google+** | Go to your Google+ page, click on 'Home' and 'Pages' and 'Create a page'. |
| **Instagram** | You can only create an Instagram account using the app on your iOS or Android device. To sign up for an Instagram account, download the Instagram app in the App Store for your iPhone/iPad, or in Google Play for an Android device. Once the app is installed, tap the Instagram icon to open it. Tap 'Register'. Create a username and password and fill out your profile info. Tap 'Done'. |
| **LinkedIn** | Open LinkedIn and select 'Companies' from the top menu. Click 'Add a Company' in the top right area of the page and enter your company's official name and your work email address. LinkedIn will send you an email to confirm. When received and confirmed, add your company information. |
| **Pinterest** | Go to **http://business.pinterest.com/setup/** and follow the on-screen instructions. |
| **Twitter** | Go to **https://twitter.com/** and click on 'New to Twitter? Sign up'. Make sure the 'Full name' is your company name. |

| SOCIAL CHANNEL | INSTRUCTIONS |
|---|---|
| YouTube | Go to **www.youtube.com** and click 'Create Account'. You will be taken to a page to create a new Google Account (Google owns YouTube). During the account sign-up process, you will be asked to specify a date of birth, gender and country. While this information is required to sign up, YouTube does not display your gender on your channel page, and you can configure your YouTube account settings so that the age and country are not displayed either. The last page of the account sign-up process will display a button linking back to YouTube. Once you are back on YouTube, click the name associated with your account and then click the 'My Channel' link to select a channel name. After creating your account, send your YouTube username to your Google Account Team and request that your account be converted to a brand channel. |

**See also**
Q26    What are the key elements of a social company page?
Q27    Do we need one central page or multiple local country pages?
Q28    How can our company page be listed in multiple industries?
Q30    How do I manage social company pages?

## Q30    How do I manage social company pages?

Managing social pages usually involves getting other people to help. There are three ways to manage most pages:

- Sign up for third party applications such as Hootsuite or Tweetdeck and share the user name. You also can sign up for 'team member' versions for an additional monthly fee.

- Share user name and passwords for individual channels.

- Add extra admins, which is available on some channels.

| SOCIAL CHANNEL | MANAGE *VIA* THIRD PARTY APPS | MANAGE ON THE PAGE |
|---|---|---|
| **Facebook** | Yes, can be managed *via* Buffer, Hootsuite. | Can add additional admins as long as they 'like' the page. |
| **Google+** | Yes but limited to six apps: Hootsuite, Buddy Media, Context Optional, Hearsay Social, Involver and Vitrue. | Admins can only be those connected to you (or connected to the primary admin). |
| **Instagram** | Available on Hootsuite Premium and Enterprise. | Only works *via* the apps. |
| **LinkedIn** | Groups and company can be managed *via* third parties. | Admins can only be those connected to you (or connected to the primary admin). |
| **Pinterest** | Not yet. | Can add other people to be pinners for specific boards. |
| **Twitter** | Yes, can be managed *via* Buffer, Hootsuite, Tweetdeck. | Probably best managed *via* third party apps as the alternative is to share the user name and password for the Twitter account. |

| SOCIAL CHANNEL | MANAGE *VIA* THIRD PARTY APPS | MANAGE ON THE PAGE |
|---|---|---|
| YouTube | Not yet. | Up to 50 people can have admin access to a YouTube channel. Google+ users can also become admins of multiple channels. Connect your YouTube channel to your Google+ page and add their team members as managers to that page. |

Access to the social channels is based on whether the channels share some code called the API (Application Programming Interface). Pinterest is restricting access at the moment, although this could change in the future.

**See also**
Q26    What are the key elements of a social company page?
Q27    Do we need one central page or multiple local country pages?
Q28    How can our company page be listed in multiple industries?
Q29    How do I set up social company pages?

# Q31    What is SoLoMo and why does it matter?

SoLoMo is a combination of SOcial media, LOcation-aware software and the use of MObile technology.

Across Europe, for every 100 inhabitants, there are 125 mobile subscriptions – some countries have fewer, but in other countries many people own more than one mobile device. Your customers are likely to own at least one form of smart mobile device and to rely on mobile technology to perform day-to-day tasks such as shopping, viewing the news, buying tickets, paying for parking and more.

Here are some reasons why SoLoMo matters:

- The top three uses for smart mobile devices are Internet browsing, email and social networking.
- Facebook, over any other social network, has the greatest impact on consumer's buying behaviour.
- 18% of smartphone users regularly use location-based apps and services to find a local retail outlet.
- 20% of Google searches involve location information.

This can be applied to your business if you:

- Sell online and customers can login to your website *via* the social networks (login *via* Facebook or Twitter). You can sell more if people see their friends have 'liked' your page.
- Are geographically fixed (food services, tourism, transport). You can promote offers to visitors and regular customers.
- Perform a local service (book a cab, find nearest store). Consider developing an app that adds value to your business for customers seeking your service.

Think about the number of times you've arrived somewhere new or in a city centre, taken out your mobile and searched for a service 'near me now'. You're part of the SoLoMo revolution too!

**See also**

Q3      What are the key social marketing channels for B2C?
Q4      What are the key social marketing channels for B2B?
Q32     What is location-based marketing?
Q60     Why does mobile matter and what should we do?

## Q32    What is location-based marketing?

Location-based marketing (LBM) is the 'place' element of the marketing mix based on mobile technology. It uses customers' locations to promote products or services.

It can be PUSH marketing where notifications are sent to the customer – for example, messages sent *via* Bluetooth when the customer is near a specific location – or PULL marketing where the customer retrieves information based on their location – for example, using the TripAdvisor® app to find restaurants 'near me now' or Foursquare to 'check-in'.

To make LBM work, the customer:

- Needs a smartphone.
- Must enable GPS.
- Might enable Bluetooth.
- May enable 'push notifications' from app developers.
- May 'social share' your location.

Location-based marketing is often used for travel, food, vouchers and tourism. Mercedes-Benz has taken this one stage further where the in-car sat nav shows restaurants, coffee shops and petrol stations *en route*.

**See also**
**Q31**    What is SoLoMo and why does it matter?
**Q60**    Why does mobile matter and what should we do?

## Q33 What types of digital marketing campaign tools are available?

The key digital campaign tools are:

- Websites.
- Email.
- Blogs.
- Online ads.
- Social networks.
- Online surveys.
- Mobile apps.

Inside each of these is a rich seam of sub-tools, for example:

- **Websites:** Regular websites, ecommerce sites, landing pages.
- **Email:** Newsletters to customers, email offers, news.
- **Blogs:** Writing on your own blog, contributing comments to others, guest posting.
- **Online ads:** Pay per click, shopping ads, sponsored ads.
- **Social networks:** From Facebook to Twitter, LinkedIn to Vine, there is a social network for all types of customers using words, images, voice and movies.
- **Online surveys:** To promote new products, gain feedback on current services and explore new opportunities.
- **Mobile apps:** To offer daily deals, exclusive previews or special access.

**See also**

Q3    What are the key social marketing channels for B2C?
Q4    What are the key social marketing channels for B2B?
Q17   Which social networks should I link up to?
Q18   What are social apps?
Q21   What are the principles of managing media online?

**Q77**  How do we measure a digital campaign?

**Q78**  How do we monitor a digital campaign?

## Q34    What are the key stages in a digital campaign?

Successful campaigns are planned, monitored, measured and reviewed. You should follow these steps to create a successful campaign.

| STAGES | ACTIONS |
| --- | --- |
| Objectives | Set SMART objectives about what you want to achieve. Who's your target audience? |
| Assets | Assemble your assets: words, images and video. |
| Plan | Create a plan: how long the campaign will run for, when and how? |
| Execute | Organise implementation of the plan. This could involve scheduling key elements in advance, such as scheduling emails, blog posts or Facebook updates. |
| Monitor | Watch, measure and review the results. Adapt as needed. |

**See also**
Q33    What types of digital marketing campaign tools are available?

## Q35    How can we create a viral campaign?

A campaign becomes viral because people find it amusing or entertaining. Campaigns are often not intended to be viral but can become so, as they are shared amongst a wide audience.

For any campaign:

- Think about the big idea – what are you trying to say?
- Who is your target audience?
- What's the message?
- What's the emotional factor?
- And the medium?

Key ingredients of a viral campaign are:

- **Surprise:** I didn't expect that!
- **Heart-warming:** Content that touches the heart and makes you feel good.
- **Animals:** Anything with cats and dogs, especially with voice-overs, seems to entertain!
- **Celebrities:** They already have a following, so using them to communicate your message can go viral, but with a large price tag outside the reach of most small businesses.

One of the most watched viral videos is 'Charlie bit my finger'. It's a home movie where a dad films his two boys, one bites the other, he finds this amusing and shares with friends *via* YouTube. So far the family has earned over half a million dollars from the video, which is funding the education for all their children.

**See also**
**Q33**    What types of digital marketing campaign tools are available?
**Q34**    What are the key stages in a digital campaign?

# Q36     How often should we post or update

The ideal frequency for posting or updating depends on your target audience. This table shows the optimum update frequency. However, if you've got something great to share, go ahead and post!

| SOCIAL CHANNEL | FREQUENCY OF POST | NOTE |
| --- | --- | --- |
| Facebook | Twice a week to daily. | Although Facebook recommends posting several times a day, the challenge is that you may appear too 'noisy' to your fan base and they may start to hide your updates. |
| Google + | Two or three times a week. | Similar to LinkedIn but as it's trying to be like Facebook a daily post for businesses is the ideal, although twice a week works too. |
| Instagram | Twice a week. | Instagram images are more about 'what's happening here' than having a professional image. The filters enable a simple cup of coffee on your desk to look good! |
| LinkedIn | Once to twice a week. | Too many updates are hidden by other users. One meaningful update a week is better than endless drivel! |
| Pinterest | Twice a week to daily. | The challenge is finding images to pin so frequently! |
| Twitter | At least once a day. | Twitter is probably the hungriest social medium and can be managed using third party tools (see **Q31**). |
| YouTube | Once a month to every quarter. | Posting to YouTube is more relevant when you have a video worth sharing. |

**See also**
**Q21**    What are the principles of managing media online?
**Q37**    What updates can we create?

# Q37    What updates can we create?

As all social media networks are hungry for content, it can be challenging to know what to post and share. This table gives you an idea of the different kinds of updates you can create.

| UPDATE TYPE | B2B | B2C | NOTE |
|---|---|---|---|
| Activities | ✓ | ✓ | Especially if it's interesting and there's an image attached. |
| Competitions | ✓ | ✓ | Ensure you follow the social network's rules on competitions. |
| Contract wins | ✓ | | |
| Events | ✓ | ✓ | |
| Feedback received | ✓ | ✓ | |
| Key dates | ✓ | ✓ | This can be a 'don't miss' or a countdown to a specific date. |
| New products / services | ✓ | ✓ | |
| Product reviews | | ✓ | |
| Projects / case studies | ✓ | | |
| Recent purchases | ✓ | ✓ | If your team has just purchased a new coffee machine, doughnuts or something that can be photographed, this can be a good update. |
| Recruiting | ✓ | ✓ | |
| Seasonal items | ✓ | ✓ | |
| Share expertise | ✓ | ✓ | |

**See also**

# Q38    How do we create an infographic?

You can create an infographic that represents something useful or informative for your customers with PowerPoint. Just follow these steps:

- Add a large box across one slide.
- Fill it with your corporate colour, extending across the whole slide.
- Copy and paste the colour box onto three, four or five slides.
- Add your charts, words and images, over the slides. Make these as large as possible.
- Open an image programme such as Paint.
- Create a new image.
- Add in each image.
- Line the images up together under each other.
- Save as an image.
- Share!

Alternatively you can create an infographic using these tools:

- http://infogr.am
- http://piktochart.com
- http://www.easel.ly

**See also**
**Q23**    What is an infographic?

# Q39    How do we develop personas for our business?

Personas help you to focus your business on your key target customers. For example, the Musgrave Group decided to segment the market of the independent retailer into two groups:

- The 'Trolley Shopper', who bought most of their groceries in one weekly shopping trip to the supermarket.
- The 'Basket Shopper', who made smaller purchases on a more frequent basis.

As a result, the brands, SuperValu and Centra, were created.

To develop personas for your business, you need to start by conducting research to understand:

- Who your current customers are.
- What are their needs?
- When do they shop, buy from you?
- Why?

When you understand your customers, you can start to map out personas. The next step is to test these draft personas against existing customers:

- Are the personas realistic?
- Do they represent your customers?

Next, you can build an image of the different personas and ensure your marketing messages are meaningful to this group.

Virgin Atlantic took over a year to create its four key personas, partly because it had such a wide customer-base. If you're a smaller business and you know your customers, you can start by considering your most 'typical customers'.

**See also**

Q24     What are personas and how do we use them?

## Q40    How can landing pages be used?

Websites often start with a home page, which can present confusing options for visitors. Landing pages take the visitor to a specific destination, often with a tailored offer. Landing pages are used in different ways.

| PURPOSE OF LANDING PAGE | HOW YOU CAN USE IT | EXAMPLE |
|---|---|---|
| **Transaction** | In PPC campaigns when a visitor clicks through for a specific offer. You can vary the transaction landing pages you create to see which work best. | Bloomberg Business Week uses a transaction landing page that the visitor clicks and gets taken direct to the 'buy now' page. |
| **Lead capture** | Useful for service businesses where an instant transaction cannot take place. If you're offering free information, request the visitor's details so you can start a dialogue. | Hubspot offers free eBooks as PDF downloads. |
| **Up-sell or cross-sell after registration** | When a visitor converts and gives you information, this is an opportunity to offer a trial period. | Smart Insights offers free subscribers opportunities to upgrade to paid membership. |
| **Up-sell or cross-sell after purchase** | When a visitor converts and makes a purchase, you can bring up a 'thank you' page with additional products (perhaps at a discounted price). | Amazon uses this: 'You've bought this, would you like one of these too?'. |

| PURPOSE OF LANDING PAGE | HOW YOU CAN USE IT | EXAMPLE |
|---|---|---|
| Social engagement | If you're growing your fan base, you can take visitors through to your Facebook or other social pages. | Some website pages invite you to 'Join us on' Twitter and Facebook with links to those sites. |

**See also**

**Q74**  What tools can we use to acquire leads online?

**Q75**  What tools can we use to convert leads?

**Q76**  What tools can we use to retain customers?

## Q41    What are the critical steps in online PR?

Traditional PR involved creating a press release and posting or emailing this to journalists who might be interested in the story. This was followed up with a telephone call to see how likely they would be to use the information.

Online PR involves different target audiences. It's no longer just about journalists, but includes bloggers, online PR websites and potentially your customers. Some businesses have established 'blogger outreach programmes' where they identify the bloggers who are most likely to share news relevant to their audiences.

The critical elements in online PR are:

### Words

It's essential to capture the attention of the reader in your headline and first sentence. As bloggers receive so many news releases a day, you have less than three seconds to make an impact.

### Images

Stories on blog and online PR websites gain more attention if an image is attached. There is nothing worse than a blogger having to request images. Either attach an image or a link to a selection of different images. Also consider that some bloggers use sites like Pinterest, which is image driven.

### Newsworthiness

Online or offline, a story still needs to be newsworthy! So if your company has won a new contract, why is it special? Why does it make a difference? And to whom? Think about the news angle and what makes this story worthy of publication.

### Pitching the release

Once you've created your story, the next step is to prepare an email to attract the journalist. Rather than sending the same email to many people, consider individual emails to the right target audience. Understand what they're looking for and why. This gives you a greater chance of the story being published.

If you know where you'd like your news to be published, look at the target websites and note their general style, tone and popular subject matter. Try to incorporate this in the writing of your release, as this will make it more relevant to the site and it is more likely to grab the journalists' attention.

### Sending the press release

Don't send your press release as an attachment with a short phrase saying 'see attached press release'. Make it easy for the journalist and add the content to the email so they can copy and paste.

### See also
**Q42** What should an online press release look like?

**QUICK WIN PUBLIC RELATIONS**

## Q42 What should an online press release look like?

An online press release contains key information:

- **Headline:** Short enough to fit into a Twitter update (less than 100 characters if you want this to be shared), with at least two keywords.

- **Subtitle:** More detail with keywords and web link to the relevant site.

- **First paragraph:** The overall point of the message in a standalone paragraph.

- **Other paragraphs:** The content should flow, should be standalone and should contain:
  - Keywords;
  - Links back to your website;
  - Good phrases that can be re-quoted *via* Twitter and other social media channels.

- **Following paragraphs:** Each paragraph should be able to be used on its own; it should include quotes or a short reference to a case study.

- **More information:** At the end of the press release, include your email address AND phone number. This allows the journalist to contact you for further information.

- **Image:** The release should include an image that can be shared (ensure it contains a link to your website).

**See also**
**Q41** What are the critical steps in online PR?

**QUICK WIN PUBLIC RELATIONS**

# Q43 What are the key issues when managing content online?

Content online falls into three categories: owned, earned and paid.

| ONLINE CONTENT | WHAT IT IS | HOW YOU CAN MANAGE IT |
|---|---|---|
| **Owned** | These are the channels you own, such as your website, Facebook page, Twitter accounts and other social media spaces bearing your brand. | Ensure the branding is consistent. Stay up to date with the rules. |
| **Earned** | Word-of-mouth mentions, reviews, added to lists and customers sharing your products *via* social media channels. | Thank those mentioning and reviewing you, whether positive or negative. Ensure your logo is available in a format to be downloaded and shared. |
| **Paid** | Paid advertising including PPC (see **Q64**), promoted tweets and banners. | You control what this is and where this appears. Ensure it follows your brand guidelines and takes the visitors to specific destinations (see **Q40**) |

**See also**

## Q44    How do we protect our visual and written content online?

Once your content is online, it is available for anyone to copy and share. Your web content, or information you have emailed, can be saved as text, images, slides, documents and pinned, shared, tweeted, blogged about or uploaded to other websites. Most of the time this is acceptable, but it's nice to get the credit for your work too!

There are ways for you to protect your content online, you can:

- **Request registration:** Protect downloads and make them accessible only after the visitor has registered. This is useful for free information such as white papers, ebooks, PDFs and slides.

- **Build in hyperlinks to your website:** For more information, the visitor must go to your website. This is where it's useful to create landing pages, related to the information (see **Q40**).

- **Build in your logos or branding:** To gain recognition.

- **Explain your intellectual property rules:** For example, 'please feel free to share our information but do include a link back to this page'.

- **Ask for a credit:** Explain how the information can be shared and ask for a credit if users do so.

**See also**
**Q14**    How do we protect our brand assets?
**Q40**    How can landing pages be used?
**Q43**    What are the key issues when managing content online?

## Q45    How do we re-use our content?

All social media channels are content-hungry. Think of content not just as words, but as images, videos and podcasts. When you've gone to the time and trouble of creating content, you need it to be used over and over again.

Start by planning your key content pieces for the next six or 12 months. Use the template below:

- **Content title:** 2014 Sector Survey.

- **What is the content about?** A survey about your sector, products, services.

- **What does it look like?** Survey questions and answers in a summary report.

- **How else can we use this?**
    o   Write a white paper about the findings: Add to website, downloadable from blog.
    o   Create summary in PowerPoint: Add to Slideshare, bookmark.
    o   Graphically illustrate key points as infographic: Add to Pinterest, Facebook.
    o   Film one of the team talking about the key points: Add to Pinterest, YouTube.
    o   Share links to the above over time.

**See also**
**Q43**    What are the key issues when managing content online?
**Q44**    How do we protect our visual and written content online?

# How do we create a simple Facebook app?

Apps in Facebook can be:

- A web-based app running **in** Facebook, and using functions within the Facebook platform (for example, the World Traveller Facebook app).
- A website or service **outside** Facebook that uses data from Facebook's API to receive from or send information to Facebook (for example, the Flickr photo uploader).

You might want to add apps to your Facebook page to:

- Run a competition.
- Capture fan details.
- Link to other events.

There are several apps that are ready to be added to your page, such as YouTube, Events and Notes. To add an app, follow these steps:

- Sign in as an administrator to the Page.
- Find the app you want.
- Go to the app's About Page. If the app is available, you'll see an 'Add App to Page' link in the menu under the Page's cover.
- Add to the page (this may take you back into your personal profile and back to the Page).
- When added, you can edit the app as needed.

If you are comfortable with technology, you might add these apps that can be customised to take fans direct to your website, or allow you to add specific images:

- Static iFrame app.
- Woobox.

And if you have a budget, you may consider buying ready-made apps from these providers:

- **www.shortstack.com**

- **www.northsocial.com**

**See also**
**Q18** What are social apps?
**Q47** How do we change the order of apps on our Facebook Page?

## Q47　How do we change the order of apps on our Facebook Page?

On Facebook pages, four apps are visible at a time. Except for Photos, all of these can be swapped with other apps. For example, there is no need to see the number of fans as this is visible under your company name; instead, you could show an app that includes your videos, 'house rules' or other information you'd like to share.

Start by expanding the views and apps menu and click the up arrow to the right of your page's setting button.

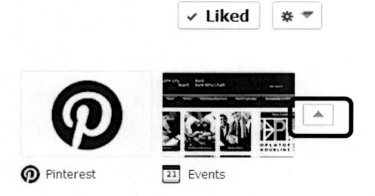

Hover over the app you'd like to swap and click the pencil icon that appears. This allows you to swap with another app on the list.

**See also**
**Q18**　What are social apps?
**Q46**　How do we create a simple Facebook app?

# Q48 Where can we demonstrate our expertise online?

In business-to-business and professional organisations, your customers are often buying your expertise. There are several social channels where you can demonstrate your skills.

| CHANNEL | WHERE YOU CAN DEMONSTRATE YOUR EXPERTISE |
|---------|-------------------------------------------|
| Google + | Ensure customers add you to relevant circles. Request reviews from customers – these link back to your Google+ page. It's quite hard work to add reviews at the moment. You need to visit **plus.google.com/local** and search for the location and locate the business to add the review. |
| LinkedIn | In your profile, add case studies, completed projects and seek recommendations. Add up to 50 areas of expertise where your connections can 'endorse' these skills. It's better to have fewer skills listed with many endorsements, than to have many skills and few endorsements. On company pages, get your products recommended by customers. |
| Quora | Answer questions about subjects in your specialist area and ask questions of experts. |
| YouTube | An opportunity to create videos demonstrating your expert knowledge. An interior designer created a 'how to fold towels like they do in hotels' video and this has received nearly half a million views! See **http://is.gd/foldtowel**. |

**See also**
**Q3** What are the key social marketing channels for B2C?

## Q49    What sales promotion activity enhances an online campaign?

Sales promotion is the process of encouraging a prospect to become a customer. It's often a temporary incentive to boost sales at an otherwise slow time.

Sales promotion techniques include:

- Offers.
- Discounts.
- Free shipping.

You might target:

| | SALES PROMOTION METHODS | |
|---|---|---|
| **CUSTOMER GROUP** | **B2C** | **B2B** |
| **Existing** | Free shipping until a specified time; €10 off voucher for all purchases over €100; free product samples with all orders placed by certain date. | Free information, downloads for all orders placed by specified time; early-bird reduced rates for events booked by certain time. |
| **Potential** | Free shipping on first order; money-off vouchers based on minimum spend. | Access to free report if visitor subscribes etc by specific time. |
| **Friends of** | Recommend a friend and both get money off next order. | Recommend a friend and both get money off next order. |

For example, Printed.Com provides a free marketing ebook to help prospects become customers (**https://www.printed.com/sign-in**). This is also a useful way to capture the prospect's email addresses.

Free marketing ebook to help you every step of the way

**Join**

**See also**

**Q10** How do we adapt our traditional brand for online marketing?
**Q75** What tools can we use to convert leads?
**Q76** What tools can we use to retain customers?

## Q50    What are the benefits of an online community?

Traditional marketing focused on one-to-one relationships, while social marketing is about one to many. Building an online community for your business is one of the best ways to reach your customers and give them a voice, especially if you sell *via* third parties. An online community makes customers feel valued and empowered. In addition, it gives you the ability to get to know them and to use that information in future product development as well as other marketing activities.

These examples show how other companies have benefited from creating online communities.

| BUSINESS / PRODUCT | HOW THEY GAIN BENEFITS FROM THEIR ONLINE COMMUNITY |
|---|---|
| Cadbury's / chocolate | New product development: Cadbury's Facebook fans requested the reinstatement of discontinued products such as the Wispa bar. |
| Barry's / tea | Encourages greater product usage *via* Facebook by sharing recipes. |
| Walker's / crisps | New product development: Walker's has engaged Facebook fans to create new flavours. |
| Tayto / crisps | Uses Facebook to announce competition winners, advertise promotions. |
| Only Marketing Jobs / jobs | Created a LinkedIn group: The UK Marketing Network - powered by www.OnlyMarketingJobs.com - has a following of around 50,000 professionals and enables the company to create brand awareness in the recruitment market, against well-known and bigger companies. |

See also
Q51    How do we build a community online?
Q52    What tools are available to create our online community?

**Q53** How do we build our online community?

**Q54** How do we manage our online community?

**Q59** What tools are available to monitor our online community?

# Q51 How do we build a community online?

Building a community online takes time. You need to be clear about your objectives and have a way to develop and nurture the community. You need strong reasons for people to join and participate as there are many established communities – for example, there are nearly two million groups in LinkedIn!

Work through this template to decide whether you should build an online community or participate in existing communities.

| QUESTION | YOUR RESPONSE |
|---|---|
| Who is your audience? | |
| What channels do they use? | |
| What are your objectives? | |
| Why will people join your community? | |
| Who will maintain the community, add fresh content and respond to questions? | |
| How often will we update the group? | |

**See also**

Q50    What are the benefits of an online community?
Q52    What tools are available to create our online community?
Q53    How do we build our online community?
Q54    How do we manage our online community?
Q55    How do we respond to online comments?
Q59    What tools are available to monitor our online community?

# Q52    What tools are available to create our online community?

When you've agreed your objectives, you can use social media networks as the tools to create your online community. The table below shows the different tools, who they're most suitable for and how to use them.

| TOOL | WHO IS IT FOR? | HOW YOU CAN USE IT | TIPS |
|------|----------------|--------------------|------|
| Blogs | B2C, B2B | Create a blog with a distinct purpose. | Add keywords into the titles of your blog posts so it's easier to find. |
| Facebook | B2C | Create a company page, invite friends and email customers to join the page. | Create a good banner image for the company's cover page. |
| LinkedIn | B2B | Create a LinkedIn group and invite connections to join. | Ensure you include information on who the group is for (geography, job type, role, etc) so that the right people join. |
| Pinterest | B2C, B2B | Create a Pinterest company page and a series of pinboards that appeal to your target audience. | Connect your Pinterest account to Facebook to increase the reach. |

**See also**

**Q3**    What are the key social marketing channels for B2C?
**Q4**    What are the key social marketing channels for B2B?
**Q50**    What are the benefits of an online community?
**Q51**    How do we build a community online?
**Q53**    How do we build our online community?
**Q54**    How do we manage our online community?

**Q59**    What tools are available to monitor our online community?

# Q53 How do we build our online community?

Once you've created the community, the next step is to **build** the community.

### Create shareable content

Communities grow when there is content worth sharing. Plan your content for the next quarter by using a spreadsheet to make an Editorial Calendar (see **Q94**).

Note that content is more than words and should include photos, images, cartoons, infographics, slideshows, PDF documents, videos and checklists. Photos and mantras (especially positive, motivational sayings) are most shared *via* Facebook, Twitter and Pinterest. Mantras or wise words are useful for B2B service companies where you may struggle to find a wide selection of images.

### Optimise your post frequency

Post frequency depends on your target customers (see **Q36**).

### Write short messages

Express your core message within the first 90 characters of your post to ensure your customers see it and to create opportunities for re-posting, retweeting, etc. Be aware that longer messages will be truncated.

### Understand your customers

Customers become fans, follow or connect for many reasons. With B2C, it's usually to gain benefits or offers. With B2B, it's to stay ahead, gather information and to be associated with your brand. Where appropriate, you can include:

- Exclusive videos.
- Competitions.
- Promotions.
- News stories.

- Discounts and offers.

**Talk to your customers**

It's important to say thank you and to give people a reason to come back and to engage – for example, through activities such as 'Fan of the Month', which works for Marmite and SodaStream.

**Promote your community**

Don't forget to share the community with your wider networks. Customers can't join your community if they don't know it exists!

**See also**

**Q50**    What are the benefits of an online community?
**Q51**    How do we build a community online?
**Q52**    What tools are available to create our online community?
**Q54**    How do we manage our online community?

# Q54    How do we manage our online community?

Once you have created your community, you need to manage it to ensure it thrives and develops.

### Rules of engagement

Clearly state who manages the page and during what times. Explain how to get customer service, if this is not available on the community page – for example, the Aer Lingus Facebook page explains how to get help:

> Welcome to the official Aer Lingus Facebook page. Please note that we're unable to respond to individual customer service issues on this page. If you require immediate assistance, please visit http://www.aerlingus.com/help/contactus/.

Snickers' Facebook page explains how it uses its fans' content:

LinkedIn groups tend to be more professional. You can add 'Rules from Group Managers', which can be automatically sent to new group members. MMC Learning, a marketing college, shares its rules with new members:

> **Rules from Your Group Managers**
>
> This is a group for MMC Learning Students who are working towards their CIM CAM Diploma in Digital Marketing. Use this group to share useful websites, books you've found and other helpful resources! If you have a specific question or concern please email your course manager directly for a quicker response.

## Moderation

There are several ways to moderate pages and groups. The detail is often in the 'Settings' area in the admin section:

- In Facebook, you can remove the 'Comments by others' in the Settings area. This can be switched on and off, so that when your team can manage the comments, this is switched on.

- In LinkedIn, you can moderate all new comments, or moderate comments from new members for a specified period of time.

## Prepare stock phrases

Twitter is more challenging as it's an open space where anyone can mention your business. Best practice is to have stock phrases ready to use when needed.

## See also

Q50    What are the benefits of an online community?
Q51    How do we build a community online?
Q52    What tools are available to create our online community?
Q53    How do we build our online community?
Q55    How do we respond to online comments?
Q59    What tools are available to monitor our online community?
Q85    How do we stop competitors commenting on our social media channels?

# Q55    How do we respond to online comments?

There is often concern that customers or competitors will say something negative about your company if there is an open, online community. This is unusual and can be managed. It's more likely that unhappy customers will share their feedback in public.

### Always respond

Many businesses only respond to negative reviews and comments. It's better to respond to both positive and negative. With positive reviews, you can thank the reviewer, as well as including extra promotional messages and your keywords – for example on TripAdvisor, Dublin's Westbury Hotel uses the hotel name, location and positive comments in a response:

> *Thank you for choosing The Westbury Hotel while visiting Dublin and for reviewing your stay on Trip Advisor. It was wonderful to read that you enjoyed your stay and thank you for your recommendations.*

With negative reviews, think carefully about the first line as this is the most visible content. Habitat manages its customer service and promotional messages *via* the same Twitter page, which means you frequently read "Sorry to hear ..." on this page. It would be better to start "My name's Annmarie and I'd like to help with these challenges ...". This shows personal responsibility as well as a willingness to resolve an issue.

### Do you need separate spaces?

If you're in a business where you receive customer care queries, it would be wise to separate the care and promotion pages. Ensure this is stated clearly on both pages, so those seeking help know where to post their messages.

### See also
Q54    How do we manage our online community?
Q85    How do we stop competitors commenting on our social media channels?

## Q56    How can marketing automation make my life easier?

Marketing automation is available for a range of tasks. Most of these have freemium versions (free but you share your details) that are suitable for smaller businesses. Enterprise paid-for versions include added benefits, such as using your own branding, managing larger numbers of customers and more admin access. The exception is sales and lead management systems which are more sophisticated all-in-one marketing systems that come with a monthly fee.

| CATEGORY | THE AUTOMATION | EXAMPLES |
|---|---|---|
| Email marketing | Issue emails, manage lists and subscribers. | Mailchimp, Constant Contact, Swiftpage, Lyris. |
| Social media publishing | Publish content at scheduled times to your social networks. | Hootsuite, Tweetdeck, Buffer. |
| Social marketing | Mine your data and advise best time to tweet, which fans to engage with more. | SocialBro. |
| Sales and lead management | Connect sales and marketing platforms: CRM, email marketing, ecommerce. | Infusionsoft, Eloqua, Marketo. |

See also
**Q57**    How do we see all our news feeds in one place?
**Q58**    How do we generate automatic content?
**Q95**    Which management tools save time?

## Q57     How do we see all our news feeds in one place?

Keeping up-to-date can be challenging! So many websites and so little time! It's easier to create 'feeds' and capture the information from the news sites of interest to you and pull these onto one page to review more easily. These news feed aggregators offer free and paid-for versions that allow you to:

- Visit a website.
- Select the feed URL.
- Add it to the aggregator.
- Label it so that you can group themes together.

Examples of feed aggregators include:

- **RebelMouse (www.rebelmouse.com):** More than a reader, this site brings together all your favourite feeds from RSS and social networks in one place, so you only have to look in one place for all your updates! The design is simple and layout is user-friendly.

- **Feedly (feedly.com):** Similar to RebelMouse, with the added value of being available as an application or extension on many mobile/tablet devices and web browsers, useful for those who access their feed on various machines.

- **NetVibes:** This freemium reader has a user-friendly dashboard.

- **Leaf:** Designed for Macs, Leaf is laid out like Twitter feed and available from the iTunes store.

Be aware that some websites have not set up feeds, so this feature is not available from all sites.

### See also
**Q56**    How can marketing automation make my life easier?
**Q58**    How do we generate automatic content?

## Q58    How do we generate automatic content?

Content curation tools make it easy to find, assemble and share content. They can be used to generate automatic content for social media or for newsletters. They are less useful for websites, as search engines like Google deem automatic content to be of low value and so they don't rank it in search results.

Three tools that offer free services are:

- Storify.
- Paperli.
- Curata.

To generate automatic content, you sign up for the service, identify the news sources you want to share, the frequency with which you wish to publish (daily, weekly) and that's it.

**See also**
**Q56**    How can marketing automation make my life easier?
**Q57**    How do we see all our news feeds in one place?

# Q59 What tools are available to monitor our online community?

Monitoring your online community enables you to:

- Say "thank you" for compliments.
- Address negative comments.
- Understand why and when your business is mentioned.
- Explore which updates generate greatest responses from your community.

Free tools to monitor your community include:

- Hootsuite.
- Tweetdeck (looks at Twitter only).

To organise monitoring, open your preferred tool and set up search streams. These could include your company name, products or brands and even your competitors. When your search terms are mentioned, you can see the results.

**See also**
Q50    What are the benefits of an online community?
Q51    How do we build a community online?
Q52    What tools are available to create our online community?
Q53    How do we build our online community?
Q54    How do we manage our online community?

# Q60　Why does mobile matter and what should we do?

Mobile usage will overtake the desktop in the next five years. This means your customers are more likely to visit your website, search for the products you offer, check out your services, *via* their mobile phone. Many people conduct searching *via* their mobile whilst at home and conclude the transaction when back at their desk. The main reason for this is that the mobile site is not yet up to the job!

This matters especially if your competitors are working on their mobile strategy. You need to take these steps:

### What's happening now?

How many of your web visitors are coming to your site *via* their mobile right now? Your Google Analytics programme will tell you.

### Check your website

Is it device-responsive or adaptive? That means does it change depending on how it's accessed? If you don't know, check it out using your mobile. Are you happy with what you see?

### Make payments easy

If you take payment online, many people won't add their credit card number on their mobile. Accept payments by PayPal or allow customers to login with a saved card.

### Integrate your marketing

Ensure your offline and online marketing are connected. Promote your mobile site offline to encourage potential customers to visit your site.

### See also
**Q31**　What is SoLoMo and why does it matter?
**Q61**　Should we have a mobile app or a mobile site?
**Q62**　What are the key issues in building a mobile app?

**Q63** What questions should we ask an agency when building a mobile app?

## Q61　Should we have a mobile app or a mobile site?

When building an app, the essential issue is that it must have a purpose; that may be to be useful, to be fun, to connect people or to provide benefits. Think about apps you use and why you use them. Which of these functions does it fulfil?

If the 'app' you are considering does not fulfil one of these functions, it is unlikely to succeed. More importantly, the largest app store, iTunes, may reject your app if it cannot see added value for its customers. Many businesses don't realise that Apple rejects many apps every day.

If your business simply wants to give customers access to a mobile version of the website, organise a 'device-responsive' website that adapts to desktops, tablets or mobile phones. It will be cheaper!

**See also**
Q31　What is SoLoMo and why does it matter?
Q60　Why does mobile matter and what should we do?
Q62　What are the key issues in building a mobile app?
Q63　What questions should we ask an agency when building a mobile app?

## Q62    What are the key issues in building a mobile app?

To build an app requires time and money. Ensure you have a budget allocated from the start and that you're clear about what you want to achieve.

Issues to consider include:

- Don't make your users guess and give it a proper name! Think about where the app appears in any directory as many are still alphabetical.

- Graphics are often very small, so great ideas on a large screen can seem fantastic, until they are shrunk to fit a mobile screen.

- If you are successful, you need to be prepared for apps to grow. This means more hosting and you may wish to explore whether your hosting company can deliver this.

- Many free apps are supported with advertising. Think ahead as to the target audience and what is and isn't acceptable.

The app development process takes a number of steps and time. Allow around three months from start to finish as your developers work through these steps:

- Brief.
- Wireframe.
- Visuals.
- Programming.
- Testing.
- Debugging.
- Testing.
- Debugging.
- Submit to directory.
- Launch.

- Promote.
- Update.

**See also**

# Q63 What questions should we ask an agency when building a mobile app?

To recruit an agency to build your app, some useful questions to ask include:

| QUESTION | RATIONALE |
| --- | --- |
| Which apps have you created? | To understand their skills and expertise. |
| What were the objectives of these apps and have they been met? | To see how well they work with customers and if a good brief had been prepared. |
| What were the main challenges? | There are always challenges! The scope can change, requirements alter, it's how they deal with these issues that's important. |
| What would you do differently? | This demonstrates how well they learn and if they improve their performance based on past experience. |
| Can we call the customers for a reference? | To check they have customers and to verify some of their work! People say more over the telephone than in an email. You can ask 'would you use this company again' and can gauge the response more easily over the phone. |
| How could the hosting work? | Are they big enough to provide hosting? Is this something they've considered? |
| What's the current timescale for approving new apps? | This is to see their current work schedules as well as checking that they understand the approval process. |

It's really important that the app easily adapts for different platforms: iPhone, Android and Windows phones. If not, you're paying for three lots of app development.

**See also**

Q31    What is SoLoMo and why does it matter?
Q60    Why does mobile matter and what should we do?
Q61    Should we have a mobile app or a mobile site?
Q62    What are the key issues in building a mobile app?
Q100   How do we engage an external agency?

# GENERATING
# SALES

# Q64    What are the key components of SEO?

Search engine optimisation (SEO) ensures your website is presented to the searcher ahead of other websites.

When you look for information in search engines like Google, the results are presented in a search engine results page (SERP) that delivers the most relevant and recent results based on SEO or paid-for adverts.

The key components of SEO are:

| COMPONENT | EXPLANATION |
|-----------|-------------|
| **Keywords** | Using keywords or key phrases that searchers will use to find your product or service is essential. |
| **Meta tags** | Search engines look at your description of the page, which is created in the meta tags. |
| **Relevant links** | Good quality links, where other websites mention your site, are essential. Never buy links or include links that have no relevance to your business or search engines will penalise your website and reduce its ranking. |
| **Quality content** | Great content includes key phrases and information for web visitors. It's essential that new content is added on a regular basis. |
| **Social media** | Connecting your social presence adds value to your website, as it widens the online footprint of your business. |

**See also**
**Q65**    How do we check our website for SEO?
**Q66**    How do we build SEO into our content?
**Q67**    How do we find the best keywords for our business?

## Q65    How do we check our website for SEO?

The quickest way to check your website for SEO is to use an automated tool. This will check your website headings, keywords, meta tags, relevant links, content and social media links. It also may give you a comparison to similar websites.

Three easy-to-use tools that don't need registration that provide you with a response in minutes are:

| TOOL | NOTES |
|------|-------|
| www.woorank.com | Gives a comprehensive review of what's working, what's not and what you need to fix. |
| www.goingup.com/analyzer | A basic tool that gives an overview only. |
| www.scrubtheweb.com | The meta analyser gives information on your meta tags and whether they're good, acceptable or bad. It's a useful place to start. |

**See also**
**Q64**    What are the key components of SEO?
**Q66**    How do we build SEO into our content?
**Q67**    How do we find the best keywords for our business?

## Q66    How do we build SEO into our content?

Once you have analysed your website and have checked out the SEO gaps, the next stage is to build in SEO opportunities.

Websites need content on a regular basis to stay 'recent' but it's not just about writing content, it's about including:

- Your keywords.

- Your products or services, as described by your customers since these are potentially the most popular keywords!

- Images that can be re-pinned with links back to your website.

- Links to relevant sites that may link back or mention your website.

- Opportunities to share the content *via* social media.

Dunelm Mill, a fast-growing UK soft furnishings supplier, faces competition for its made-to-measure curtains. Whilst it invests in online ads (see **Q64**), it has built in SEO, using the words curtain, curtains and many variations, as shown here:

**Curtains**

Hundreds of design and fabric combinations make up our gorgeous collection of black curtains, all conveniently ready to hang and available in a range of sizes. As a decorative and functional home accessory your drapes are a detail worth getting right, which is why we also offer a Made to Measure curtains service.

As well as a wide range of eyelet and pencil pleat curtains, Dunelm offers net curtains and beaded curtains, providing privacy without blocking out sunlight. We also have a selection of luxury curtains, including the soft and elegant touch of our Chenille curtains range.

Whether you require drapes for your bedroom or a new set of living room curtains, colour is often an important consideration. For an opulent finishing touch, consider the rich tones of our purple curtains or plum curtains. You may also enjoy the glamorous shine our silver curtains and gold curtains will bring to your living environment. Our beautiful teal curtains or blue curtains will also present a subtle influence.

**See also**

Q64     What are the key components of SEO?
Q65     How do we check our website for SEO?
Q67     How do we find the best keywords for our business?

## Q67 How do we find the best keywords for our business?

One of the challenges with marketing online is that one in every 20 searches is unique. That's 5% of all searches *via* Google. One of the reasons for this is that we are becoming more sophisticated and instantly seeking better search results. If we are looking for a holiday, we are unlikely to search for 'holiday' but more likely to use 'long tail keywords' such as 'holiday warm in October fly from Cork' or 'holiday villa with children, pool in Italy near Pisa'.

Added to this, customers often use different keywords to those that you may consider. Start by looking through your Google Analytics results to see which words customers are using to find you. What are the most popular terms? Any surprises?

You also can analyse your keywords using an automated tool, to see what keywords are found on your website. Use these tools to look at your competitors' websites to see what works well for them!

Tools include:

- **Google Keyword Planner (was Keyword Tool):** This will show you the average monthly searches, advertising competition for the keyword and the cost per click if you chose to advertise. It's a free tool and to access it you need a Google account.

- **www.wordstream.com/keywords:** Another free tool, this website allows you to suggest your keywords and will recommend others.

**See also**
**Q64**  What are the key components of SEO?
**Q65**  How do we check our website for SEO?
**Q66**  How do we build SEO into our content?

# Q68 What is pay per click (PPC) advertising?

Pay per click (PPC) is online advertising where you pay every time someone clicks on your advert on a search engine or other website.

The advert might be shown on a desktop PC, tablet or mobile. It may be promoted as an ad or as 'Sponsored Links'.

To get started, sign up for an account with a search engine such as Google or Bing, create an advert and bid (like in an auction) on keywords. The more you pay, the more likely you are to get to the top of the page.

As with any auction, the fees depend on your keywords and their popularity as well as your website's own online reputation, which Google refers to as a 'Quality Score'. So those with better quality scores can pay less!

Costs per click vary (CPC) and, as an example, for low popularity key words can be 50 cent to €5, and for more popular ones you can expect an average CPC of €7+.

The advantages and disadvantages of PPC:

| ADVANTAGES | DISADVANTAGES |
|---|---|
| It's fast to set up, much quicker than developing an organic SEO strategy. | It can be expensive to secure the keywords you really want. |
| You can be seen outside Google; if your ads are in the 'Google Ad Network', you can appear on blogs and other companies' pages. | You may appear on blogs and other pages that you don't want (but there is a degree of control to ensure this doesn't happen). |
| You can set a daily, weekly or monthly budget. | It needs managing daily. |
| Low competition keywords can be cheaper to access. | Click fraud can occur, so beware! |

**See also**
**Q69**  What is social advertising?

**Q70** What budget should we set for online advertising?

**Q71** What is remarketing?

## Q69    What is social advertising?

Pay per click (PPC) is primarily concerned with search engines like Google and is re-active, advertising to a group of people based on their search terms.

Social advertising is pro-active and takes advertising one step forward, enabling you to target specific people based on your own criteria. It's a relatively new phenomenon and Twitter and Pinterest have only just started allowing advertisers to connect with target customers.

Facebook allows you to target potential customers based on:

- Location.
- Gender.
- Age.
- Interests.
- Education.
- Marital status.

As an example, a photographer offering wedding services could place ads on the Facebook pages of women, aged 25 to 28, who are recently engaged and based within an hour of the photographer's studio. LinkedIn ads enable you to target job roles and industries – for example, you could promote your business only to finance directors working in IT companies, within a 50-mile radius of your office.

Like PPC, Facebook advertising is based on an auction system. You also can set daily budgets from €10 and start and finish times for campaigns.

Twitter has different offers, including:

- Promoted Tweets aimed at larger businesses that are estimated to cost around €100,000 in the UK and Ireland.
- Promoted Trends, a 24-hour feature, with estimated current costs in the UK and Ireland around €24,000 per trend.

- Promoted Accounts that are based on a cost per follower (like cost per click) and are sold on an auction system.

**See also**
**Q68** What is pay per click (PPC) advertising?
**Q70** What budget should we set for online advertising?
**Q71** What is remarketing?

## Q70     What budget should we set for online advertising?

There are two approaches to online advertising: you can opt for a 'Do It Yourself' approach or engage an agency. The budget depends on the time you have available and the approach you take. There isn't an upper limit as some companies find most of their business is driven *via* web traffic from Google, so the more they spend, the more traffic they generate.

If you're opting for DIY, you can allocate smaller budgets, from €500 per month for PPC. You need to set up a Google account and follow the online instructions. The ads are likely to cost more as you have less buying power.

Working with an agency, you need to consider at least €15,000 a year. Small agencies might allow you to work on a monthly basis, spending €1,250 per month. You'll find larger agencies with more skills are more likely to organise five tranches of say €3,000 at times of year that are more critical to your business.

**See also**
**Q68**    What is pay per click (PPC) advertising?
**Q69**    What is social advertising?

# Q71   What is remarketing?

Remarketing is a new form of online advertising. It's also known as 'follow me marketing' or re-targetting and it provides adverts to people who may have searched for the term earlier that day on a specific computer, once more.

Suppose someone searches on Google for, say, 'fruit basket' and based on the search results visits the Marks & Spencer website. Later that day, another advert promoting 'fruit baskets from M&S' is delivered to the searcher. Google is working on the basis that several searches have taken place and the searcher hasn't found what they're looking for.

Correctly set up in Google, remarketing allows you to target searchers who have visited your website with additional promotional images *via* other websites who have signed up to the Google Ad Network.

The downsides are that the searcher may:

- Already have made the purchase and be irritated by being followed around.
- Not accept cookies in which case they can't be targeted.

**See also**
**Q68**   What is pay per click (PPC) advertising?
**Q69**   What is social advertising?

## Q72    How do we attract followers?

When you're starting out and building your social footprint, it's harder to get followers as you don't seem established. Followers will follow you if:

- They get a benefit.
- It is useful for them.
- It's fun.
- Their friends follow you.

| BRAND / ORGANISATION | CHANNEL | WHY FANS FOLLOW |
|---|---|---|
| Easons Ireland | Facebook | **Benefit:** To hear about book signings. |
| Brown Thomas | Facebook | **Friends follow:** With nearly 90,000 fans, most of your friends will be following. |
| Marmite | Facebook | **Fun:** Sharing photos of Marmite, swapping recipes ... |
| Shelbourne Hotel | Twitter | **Useful:** Instant customer service. |
| MalMaison Birmingham | Twitter | **Benefit:** They promote offers. |

Think about your business and what it can offer. Who are your customers? If B2B, it's often about being useful and offering benefits such as free white papers, new information or being 'first to hear'.

**See also**
**Q73**    How do we get more fans, followers and likes?

## Q73 How do we get more fans, followers and likes?

Likes, fans and followers are acquired when you meet your customers' needs. There are specific actions on the different networks:

| TOOL | ACTION TO GET MORE FANS, FOLLOWERS, LIKES, ETC |
|------|------------------------------------------------|
| Facebook | Get a good page together: Fill in all the basics and organise good cover pages.<br>Tell your customers you're on Facebook; promote it on all printed material, everywhere you connect with customers; add Facebook Fanbox / Like to your website.<br>Use your keywords in profile, updates; tag photos with keywords, product names.<br>Facebook has dedicated advertising packages (see **Q64** and **Q65**). |
| Google+ | Get your page ready: add some content, regular updates and link back to your website.<br>Use keywords in the updates.<br>Find other people to add to your circles – they may follow back. |
| LinkedIn | LinkedIn isn't a business card competition, connect with care. Make sure your existing customers know you're using the network and invite them to connect. For your Company Page, organise some content, update regularly and tell your network about the page. |
| Pinterest | Promote your page on all printed material, everywhere you connect with customers.<br>Add a Pinterest connect button to your website.<br>Use your keywords in profile, updates; tag photos with keywords, product names. |

| TOOL | ACTION TO GET MORE FANS, FOLLOWERS, LIKES, ETC |
|------|------------------------------------------------|
| **Twitter** | Be polite! Thank new followers and people who mention you. Their followers see this and some will check you out and also may follow you. |
| | Be focused on your subject; others may be searching for this area and will find you. Use #hashtags about your subject. |
| | Create lists (either public or private) and add groups of customers. They can see they've been added to the list and at this stage become aware of you. |
| | Find out event/conference #hashtags before attending and use them to identify others attending and mention them, follow before the event. |
| | Ask to be re-Tweeted: 'pls RT'. |

**See also**

Q3    What are the key social marketing channels for B2C?
Q4    What are the key social marketing channels for B2B?
Q33   What types of digital marketing campaign tools are available?
Q34   What are the key stages in a digital campaign?
Q72   How do we attract followers?

## Q74 What tools can we use to acquire leads online?

Your website is your primary lead acquisition tool and ideally all traffic should be directed back to this. You can ensure your website works effectively (see **Q84**), buy advertising (see **Q64**) and/or take action in the social networks:

| TOOL | ACTION TO ACQUIRE LEADS |
|------|--------------------------|
| **Facebook** | Encourage interaction and sharing so the 'friends of' also see your posts, increasing your audience size and the potential for new customers.<br>Organise number countdowns (only 5 more till 1,000 fans, etc).<br>Create useful, interesting content that will be shared.<br>Time-limited competitions can be used to generate leads and convert leads into sales. |
| **Google+** | Create a Google hangout; set a time and date to discuss an issue to showcase your knowledge. Hangouts can be public and anyone can join in and see you and your screen online. |
| **LinkedIn** | Listen, build connections, provide updates and offers to them.<br>Reconnect with past customers who may have moved on, but still have an interest in your product or service.<br>Use advanced search to explore contacts within companies and make direct contact with potential customers.<br>Identify potential customers, explore the 'degrees of separation' between connections and ask for an introduction.<br>Connect to potential customers before initial meetings so they can check your profile and identify areas of common interest.<br>Add a SlideShare application to upload brochures, presentations. Your connections will see the updates and if relevant to them, they may get in touch.<br>Look at your customer segments – find relevant groups and get involved. |
| **Pinterest** | Create useful, interesting images that will be shared.<br>Don't forget videos can be added to Pinterest! |

| TOOL | ACTION TO ACQUIRE LEADS |
|------|-------------------------|
| Twitter | Create your own #hashtags around your campaigns – for example, Smart Insights, the digital marketing consultancy, uses the hashtag #plantosucceed to get noticed in Twitter. Ensure your product or service can be found. Include the relevant keywords for your product or service with details of how to contact you in your 'bio'. |
| Website | Include 'calls to action' on your website; your telephone number, contact details, newsletter sign-ups and downloads accessed by filling in a form that contains the prospect's details. |

**See online**

Q3      What are the key social marketing channels for B2C?
Q4      What are the key social marketing channels for B2B?
Q64     What are the key components of SEO?
Q73     How do we get more fans, followers and likes?
Q75     What tools can we use to convert leads?
Q76     What tools can we use to retain customers?
Q84     Which tools can we use to review our competitors' websites?

## Q75 What tools can we use to convert leads?

Lead conversion is enhanced with online automated systems (see **Q56**). These are additional steps you can take in the different networks.

| TOOL | ACTION TO CONVERT LEADS TO SALES |
|------|----------------------------------|
| **Facebook** | Organise Facebook only announcements and offers. Any offers must follow Facebook's T&Cs.<br>Add a review plugin onto your Facebook page, so others can see what their friends have reviewed. |
| **LinkedIn** | Use the LinkedIn message system to send one-to-one messages about a product or service that may be of interest.<br>Nurture your network, stay in touch. |
| **Pinterest** | Add the shopping cart URL in all product images. |
| **Twitter** | Ask questions of your followers to understand why they are following.<br>Provide time-limited offers. These don't need to be financial, they can be exclusive access, for the first 100, or this month only, or a limited edition. |
| **Website** | Having captured prospects' details *via* email or newsletter sign-ups, send out a regular newsletter containing information they are likely to find useful or interesting. This may include time-limited offers.<br>If yours is a B2B company, send invites to events, conferences, exhibitions so you get a chance to meet prospects face-to-face.<br>Invite them to connect *via* LinkedIn so you can get to know each other. |

**See also**
**Q56**   How can marketing automation make my life easier?
**Q74**   What tools can we use to acquire leads online?
**Q76**   What tools can we use to retain customers?

## Q76    What tools can we use to retain customers?

It's often quoted that the cost of acquiring a new customer is six to seven times more than keeping existing customers. Customer satisfaction is a key driver in repurchasing. Happy customers will buy from you again, unhappy ones won't – unless they have no choice.

To retain existing customers:

- Talk to them!
  - o If there are large numbers of customers, conduct regular surveys to find out if they are unhappy with any aspect of the business (see **Q90**).
  - o If there are a few relatively close to your office, do the old fashioned thing and visit them!
  - o If they are further afield, use Google Hangouts or Skype. Simply get a Google or Skype account, a webcam and get started. A call with video is more meaningful as you can see the facial expressions.

- Share your news:
  - o If you have news, if you're changing the way something works, tell existing customers about it first. There's nothing worse than being the last to find out when you're a loyal customer.
  - o Give plenty of notice about changes in prices. Don't justify why there's an increase, keep the message simple and let them know when this will happen.

- Reward your customers:
  - o A reward doesn't need to be financial: it could be free samples, invitations to take part in product trials or invitations to join you for an event.
  - o Rewards also can be recognition: Marmite, a savoury spread, has developed its Facebook fan page and rewards its most ardent online customers by promoting them as 'fan of the month' with their name and photo appears on the Marmite fan page for a month.

- o RS Components has created a community blog for its fans **www.designspark.com,** which it calls *"the gateway* to online resources and design support for engineers".
- o Financial rewards such as discounts can teach customers to wait until there is another discount or offer before they shop. If you do provide a discount, ensure it's not on a regular basis.

- Loyalty programmes: To encourage customers to buy from you after an initial purchase, loyalty programmes can be effective, as long as the customer is satisfied with their purchase! Programmes can include:
  - o Benefits: Free shipping, or free next day delivery.
  - o Discounts: A percentage off their next order or a discount in your slower months, as long as a minimum spend is met.
  - o Points that can be exchanged for goods.
  - o Before embarking on a loyalty programme explore whether they are satisfied and whether a reward would be a better fit for your business.

**See also**
**Q74** What tools can we use to acquire leads online?
**Q75** What tools can we use to convert leads?
**Q90** How can we survey our customers online?

# MEASURING, MONITORING & MANAGING

# Q77    How do we measure a digital campaign?

It's challenging to run a digital campaign without setting goals in advance. To measure and monitor a digital campaign, you need to:

- Set objectives before you start! Decide what you want to achieve; more visitors to the website, more sales *via* the website – be specific.
- Be realistic – doubling web sales may not achievable or manageable! Ensure the objectives can be accomplished.

Ways to measure digital success include those listed below. Take a measure of your current situation and compare.

- Views (videos, ads, rich images).
- Fans, Likes, Followers.
- Sharing, re-tweets.
- Favourites.
- Email subscriptions.
- Group membership.
- Downloads.
- Bookmarks.
- Ratings, Reviews, Love, Like this.
- Number of visitors to owned media (i.e. web traffic).
- Conversion rate on your website.
- Sales.
- Repeat sales.

**See also**
Q34    What are the key stages in a digital campaign?
Q78    How do we monitor a digital campaign?
Q79    How do we monitor brand conversations?
Q80    What are the key measures we should use?

# Q78    How do we monitor a digital campaign?

Monitoring a digital campaign requires some work to set up a dashboard, or gather initial information. The table below shows how different campaigns can be monitored.

| DIGITAL CAMPAIGN | TOOL TO DELIVER CAMPAIGN | HOW TO MONITOR |
|---|---|---|
| **Email** | Mail Chimp, Constant Contact. | Dashboard provides campaign statistics: number of opens, clickthroughs. |
| **Pay per click (PPC)** | Google Adwords. | Increased traffic to website and increased sales. |
| **Building group in communities like LinkedIn** | No tool to build, need to achieve *via* LinkedIn profile. | Number of members meeting criteria for group membership. |

Once you have set up your dashboard, you can monitor different campaigns over time. This shows you which campaigns worked best and why, enabling you to get better results.

**See also**
**Q34**    What are the key stages in a digital campaign?
**Q77**    How do we measure a digital campaign?
**Q79**    How do we monitor brand conversations?

## Q79    How do we monitor brand conversations?

Businesses are keen to see who is talking about their business or specific brands. Monitoring tools range from fairly basic and free like Google or Giga Alerts to more sophisticated and paid-for, like Raven tools.

Whatever the tool you select, some intervention is still required to take follow-up action! If your brand is mentioned positively, you may need to thank or compliment the feedback. If the feedback or comments are negative, you need to address the issues as quickly as possible.

| TOOL | NOTE |
|------|------|
| **Hootsuite, Tweetdeck** | Set up streams to see when and where the business is mentioned. |
| **www.gigaalert.com** | Free tool that allows you to set up an alert to see when and where the business is mentioned (this used to be Google Alerts). |
| **SocialBro** | Identifies your advocates and who you influence; enables you to start conversations direct with those individuals. |
| **www.trackur.com** | A paid-for tool, starting at $27 per month and identifies positive and negative sentiment about your brand. |
| **Raven's social monitoring tool** | A paid-for tool from $99 per month that covers all social media mentions (see **http://raventools.com/tools/social-media-monitor**). |

**See also**
**Q10**    How do we adapt our traditional brand for online marketing?
**Q78**    How do we monitor a digital campaign?

# Q80    What are the key measures we should use?

The key measures fall into three areas:

| MEASUREMENT AREA | WHAT'S MEASURED |
| --- | --- |
| **Tracking metrics** | Visitors.<br>Source of traffic.<br>Conversion to action rates. |
| **Performance drivers** | Number of fans compared to competitors.<br>Cost per click, quality score.<br>Compliments, positive reviews. |
| **Business value** | New and repeat sales.<br>Volume of recommendations and reviews. |

It's likely that you will use at least one measure in each area at some stage. If you're developing a new website, the initial measure will be the number of visitors. When your website is better established, you may measure the sales generated online. The essential step is to ensure you measure an aspect of your business that is meaningful to you.

**See also**
**Q77**    How do we measure a digital campaign?
**Q81**    How can we measure our social influence?

# Q81    How can we measure our social influence?

As social media has become more important to business, measurement tools have been created that measure the impact or influence you're having online. It also enables individuals to establish their credibility and expertise in specific areas.

The three key tools are Klout, PeerIndex and Kred.

All the tools start by getting you to link up the social channels where you have a presence. The scores are calculated by aggregating over 400 different signals in each individual's social media activity – for example, how many times a tweet is shared, someone likes a comment or mentions you in a post.

Salesforce recently advertised for a new community manager and listed "Klout score 35 or higher" as a desired skill for the position. It is not the only company to put a great deal of weight on a candidate's Klout score, with one company reportedly cutting short an interview with a person who had 15 years' experience working with established companies simply because his Klout score was only 34. They went on to hire someone with a score of 67.

Whilst not everyone consider these scores essential, it raises your profile and shows how your social activity is having an impact on your community.

**See also**
**Q2**     What is the impact of 'social' on the marketing mix?
**Q11**    How do we assess our digital strengths and weaknesses?
**Q77**    How do we measure a digital campaign?
**Q78**    How do we monitor a digital campaign?
**Q79**    How do we monitor brand conversations?
**Q80**    What are the key measures we should use?

# Q82 How do we benchmark our social marketing against competitors?

This template is designed to compare and contrast your social marketing against your competitors. Work through each step for your key competitors and don't forget to include your own business too!

| QUESTION | BENCHMARKING | RESPONSE |
|---|---|---|
| **Which channels?** | Which social networks are used and for what? | |
| **Who is updating?** | Is it an internal team, external agency or a mix? You can usually tell as an agency can push a lot of updates at the same time. Or if it's in-house, they often specify the names of those working on the account. | |
| **When updating?** | Monday to Friday only or more? Does it fit with customers' needs? | |
| **Latest update?** | Can you explore their activity? Are the accounts still current? Did they start with good intentions and abandon some networks? | |
| **Contribution?** | What's the number and type of updates? For example, sales messages, competitions, photos, interaction? | |
| **No of fans, likes?** | What's the following to date? (see **Q72**) | |
| **Programmes used?** | What's the integration between social media tools? Are updates *via* Hootsuite or something else? Are all their updates the same? This shows how they are managing their networks. | |

| QUESTION | BENCHMARKING | RESPONSE |
|---|---|---|
| Links to landing pages? | Where are fans directed? To the main website home page or to a dedicated Facebook landing page? | |
| Identity format? | Do they use a corporate face? Brand identity? Or individuals within the company? Which works best in this sector? | |

**See also**

Q83    What tools can we use to reveal our competitors online strategies?
Q84    Which tools can we use to review our competitors' websites?

## Q83　What tools can we use to reveal our competitors online strategies?

The aim of most websites is to generate leads. Generating leads online comes from effective search engine optimisation (SEO), unless a business is paying for advertising. Effective SEO is a mix of many elements, including:

- Getting traffic to the site: if your site attracts significant traffic, Google and other search engines rank the site as being important.
- The right keywords.
- Relevant backlinks to the website.

These tools give you an assessment of your competitors' online strategies:

| TOOL / SITE | HOW TO USE IT |
| --- | --- |
| **www.alexa.com** | Ideal for larger websites. This tool reviews visitor traffic, audience profile and how long visitors stay on site. Note that there is no data if your site isn't a major player. |
| **www.compete.com** | Similar to Alexa, but this tool needs larger traffic sites to work. |
| **www.google.com/trends** | Will show search volumes for specific keywords and other terms, such as product groups. If there are insufficient volumes, there are no trends to see. Google trends also shows emerging trends which is a useful tool for conducting new product research. |

| TOOL / SITE | HOW TO USE IT |
|---|---|
| **adwords.google.co.uk** | Use the keyword planner to see the keywords on your competitors' websites. You need a Google login to access this tool at any depth. This shows the competition for the keywords and their likely costs. |
| **www.wordstream.com/keywords** | Use this tool to review keywords on your competitors' websites. It's free and can search up to 30 keywords at a time. Shows the competition for the keywords and likely costs. |
| **www.opensiteexplorer.org** | Shows back links to the site. This is an indication of how well connected their website is, although Google has castigated websites with too many irrelevant links. Check to see whether the links include review websites, registers, lists or places that would be useful for your website. |

**See also**

**Q82**   How do we benchmark our social marketing against competitors?
**Q84**   Which tools can we use to review our competitors' websites?
**Q85**   How do we stop competitors commenting on our social media channels?
**Q86**   How do we monitor our competitors' activity online?

## Q84 Which tools can we use to review our competitors' websites?

These tools can be used to review any website: your own and your competitors' sites. This tells you how well they've connected their social networks, whether their website is mobile-optimised and the average time between blog posts.

| TOOL / SITE | HOW TO USE IT |
| --- | --- |
| www.woorank.com | Easy-to-use, free, website reviewer. Shows you where to improve, what's good and your social connections. |
| www.freegrader.com | Brief overview giving your website a score out of 100. Shows where improvements can be made and what works. Good as a starting point. |
| http://marketing.grader.com | Hubspot's website grader is possibly the best-known website grader and claims to have reviewed over one million websites. Today, this is a more basic overview. |

At least once a year, review your website and compare it with your competitors.

### See also
Q82 How do we benchmark our social marketing against competitors?
Q83 What tools can we use to reveal our competitors online strategies?
Q85 How do we stop competitors commenting on our social media channels?
Q86 How do we monitor our competitors' activity online?

## Q85    How do we stop competitors commenting on our social media channels?

In an online world, your competition can comment negatively about your business. However, if they post inaccurate or untrue information, this still falls under the defamation laws.

Here are some ways you can exclude your competitors or at least manage their presence in your network:

| SOCIAL CHANNEL | KEEPING COMPETITORS AT BAY |
|---|---|
| Facebook | You can add competitors' names to the blocklist box in Settings. This means any posts from or including competitors' names, won't be published. If your competitors do add comments, you can remove or report them if needed. |
| Pinterest | Your competitors can comment on images that you pin, but this is unusual. You can delete comments and delete images if needed. |
| Twitter | Competitors are unlikely to add negative comments as these can be seen by their own network. |
| YouTube | To allow comments on your channel from anyone, you need to enable the Discussion Tab. Best practice is to 'hold comments for approval'. In Channel Navigation, switch this on and a blue banner will let you know when new comments appear. You can review the comments to approve, delete, or flag them for abuse or spam. If you receive comments that you wish to remove, click on the arrow above the comment and simply remove. Note that this also removes the whole string of replies. If extreme cases, you can ban a user from your channel! |

**See also**
**Q55**    How do we respond to online comments?

## Q86    How do we monitor our competitors' activity online?

It's much easier to obtain competitor information online. To see how your competitors are performing and better understand their marketing practices, you can:

- Sign up for their newsletters to read their content and understand the frequency of issue.

- Sign up forGigaAlert, which has replaced Google Alert, to be notified when they post new information online.

- If they are listed on a stock exchange, buy some of their shares. As a shareholder you will always receive the latest news, annual reports and financial details.

- Buy some of their products from their online store. Check out their service, packaging, customer care and the product offer.

- Return products you've bought online to see how they manage the process.

- Look at their social media presence (see **Q83**) and have a good look at the photos they post (are they of staff, products, their building?) – this tells you what's really happening in the business.

- If they exhibit at large conferences and events, visit their stand and check out what's new.

You also may be in the same trade association as your competitors. Don't forget to attend meetings to hear the latest online and offline news!

**See also**
**Q83**    What tools can we use to reveal our competitors online strategies?
**Q84**    Which tools can we use to review our competitors' websites?

## Q87    Where should we gain reviews for B2C?

As online shopping has grown, we often look at the comments made by others if considering a purchase. A one-star review can turn a potential purchase into a failed purchase and a five-star review can speed up a purchase decision. Reviews, ratings and comments are here to stay and have a direct impact on sales.

As more websites adopt review systems to capture independent endorsements of their business, independent verification is essential. The following sites offer independent verification and are aimed at the B2C sector, although some B2B organisations use these tools.

| WEBSITE | WHAT THEY SAY | COSTS |
|---|---|---|
| www.trustpilot.co.uk | Trustpilot is an open, community-based platform for sharing real reviews of shopping experiences online. | From £75 per month. |
| www.feefo.com | As feefo sends a feedback request to each customer who buys from you, its packages are based on the number of sales you make per month. | Set up fee of £199 and from £99 per month based on sales volume. |
| www.reevoo.com | An independent and impartial ratings and reviews provider, working with brands like Sony, Acer, KIA, Currys, DEWALT and Kuoni. | From £499 per month. |

Travel sites are worth a mention if you're in the hospitality sector. TripAdvisor is the market leader, although it is not a verified review site. As a TripAdvisor reviewer, I could review absolutely anywhere, regardless of whether I've stayed there or not. LateRooms and Evivvo, two other travel sites, only send review invitations to people who have made a booking through their website. This ensures the feedback displayed is genuine.

**See also**

Q3      What are the key social marketing channels for B2C?
Q79     How do we monitor brand conversations?
Q88     Where should we gain reviews for B2B?

## Q88    Where should we gain reviews for B2B?

We trust personal recommendations more than any other form of advertising. Word-of-mouth (or word-of-mouse!) means more than an advert.

Business-to-business companies can use the same review sites as B2C but it's less meaningful. Many B2B companies try to win awards to demonstrate their skills.

Another route is to obtain recommendations on your LinkedIn company page, although it's easier for individual staff to obtain endorsements and recommendations.

| WEBSITE | POINTS TO NOTE |
|---|---|
| LinkedIn Company Page recommendations | These are difficult to gain. You don't know when someone has added a recommendation – you find out only when you've checked the page! You can now comment on a recommendation, flag if inappropriate or delete. |
| LinkedIn Personal Profile recommendations | You can request a recommendation from colleagues, business partners or suppliers. It's important to adapt the standard template and be specific in your request: What would you like to be recommended for? Think about your keywords and include these in the request. |
| LinkedIn Personal Profile endorsements | LinkedIn allows you to list up to 50 skills in your profile. Your network will see messages requesting that they endorse these skills. They can add other skills they think you have too. It's wise to focus on key skills that gain many endorsements instead of a long list with few endorsements. |

**See also**
**Q3**     What are the key social marketing channels for B2C?
**Q79**   How do we monitor brand conversations?
**Q87**   Where should we gain reviews for B2C?

# Q89 What are some easy ways to get customer feedback on our website?

When customers are on your website, it's a great opportunity to find out why they're there, what they're looking for and why they have (or haven't) purchased. Automated tools are the easiest way of achieving this.

Two useful tools, both paid for, are:

| WEBSITE | HOW THIS HELPS | COST |
|---------|----------------|------|
| www.qualaroo.com/ | Targets customers on your website to ask 'what's stopping you from buying now?' Lots of survey options. Aimed at retail businesses. | From $199 per month |
| www.kampyle.com/ | Feedback forms for your website so you start receiving feedback from your customers immediately. | From $249 per month |

If your website is created using WordPress, an open source solution, you could explore these free plugins that are designed to capture customer feedback:

- **http://wordpress.org/plugins/webengage**.
- **http://wordpress.org/plugins/feedweb**.
- **http://wordpress.org/plugins/wp-polls**.

**See also**
**Q90** How can we survey our customers online?
**Q91** How can we survey non-customers online?

## Q90    How can we survey our customers online?

At least once a year, it's a good idea to find out what your customers think about your products and services. The two main survey tools are **www.polldaddy.com** and **www.surveymonkey.com**. Both websites offer a free basic service and take you through the steps to create a survey with options to email a link, embed the link in an email or send links from email addresses you supply.

The main difference between the free and paid-for versions are removing their branding and adding your own, increased reporting and issuing the survey to a larger number of people.

When surveying customers, focus on the main areas of dissatisfaction rather than satisfaction. Customers leave you because they're unhappy not because they're happy.

**See also**
**Q89**    What are some easy ways to get customer feedback on our website?
**Q91**    How can we survey non-customers online?

**QUICK WIN MARKETING Q82** How do we survey existing clients?

# Q91    How can we survey non-customers online?

Non-customers don't know you and they don't know your website address. This means you need to find where they are if you want to talk to them.

For business-to-business companies, LinkedIn advertising can target non-customers by their location, job role, seniority and industry.

For business-to-consumer companies, Facebook advertising can be used to answer specific questions.

For all businesses, Google conducts surveys that are ads placed on pages when people are searching for specific words (see **www.google.com/ insights/consumersurveys/home**).

**See also**
**Q89**   What are some easy ways to get customer feedback on our website?
**Q90**   How can we survey our customers online?

## Q92    What techniques can be used to improve user experience?

The online customer/user experience has an impact on whether a customer stays on your website or moves elsewhere. If you are building a new website or improving your existing site, factors to consider to improve user experience include:

### Ask your audience

Find out what customers think about your website. Here are two websites that give you easy ways to test your web design:

| WEBSITE | HOW THIS HELPS | COST |
|---------|----------------|------|
| www.fivesecondtest.com/ | Fivesecondtest helps fine-tune your landing pages and calls to action by analysing the most prominent elements of your design. | From $20 per month |
| www.usersnap.com/ | Screenshot tool for web development. Get annotated screenshots of the current browser content, directly delivered to your bug tracker or project management tool. | From $19 per month |

### Run a usability test

Usability tests can be organised online with companies like **http://www.loop11.com**, which charges $350 for a one-off test or you can organise them in house.

What is the aim of your website? If it's for customers to buy your products on, look at options or download a paper, why not:

- Prepare a short statement saying what needs to be done.
- Recruit people who would be your typical customers.
- Ask them to carry out the action.

- And give you feedback.

You could do this using a church hall, or local coffee shop. Add in a couple of laptops and give the users something in return, say €20 for their time. Ten users will give you reasonable feedback; 20 users will probably cover all the issues.

## Review your navigation

The challenge with most websites is the navigation. The website may have started as a simple site, but after a few years, it may have grown and the navigation becomes cumbersome. Try to navigate your own site. How easy do you find it to navigate?

## Look at your analytics

If you use Google Analytics, your reports will show which pages your visitors started at and where they left. It will show the terms they are using to search within the site. How easy is it to find what they're seeking?

## Check out your competitors

How does your site compare? Who is easiest to use? (see **Q84**)

## See also

**Q83**    What tools can we use to reveal our competitors online strategies?
**Q84**    Which tools can we use to review our competitors' websites?
**Q86**    How do we monitor our competitors' activity online?

## Q93    How do we develop an online value proposition (OVP)?

Marketing used to focus on unique selling propositions (USPs). Today we refer to value propositions, which can be online value propositions (OVPs). An OVP tells your customers why they should buy from you and is usually based on price, products or service.

To develop your OVP, look at these elements within your business:

| ELEMENT | TO CONSIDER | EXAMPLE |
|---|---|---|
| **Product** | Are there opportunities for modifying the core or extended product online? | WH Smith, the stationers, selling personalised greetings cards online. |
| **Price** | There is increased transparency, downwards pressure on price and adoption of new pricing models online, so what can you do? | Amazon offers free delivery for books over a certain value. It also offers a membership service (Prime), which gives free delivery. |
| **Place** | New channels and new channel structures. | A group of London cab drivers launched Hailo, an app to book a taxi in many cities. |
| **People** | Changing role of staff and the time they're needed. | Everyone is in marketing, as admin staff move into customer care roles, answering questions in public. |
| **Promotion** | New communications methods, new client touchpoints, managing relationships, so what can your business do? | LinkedIn, Facebook and Twitter allow advertising to people based on their interests. |

| ELEMENT | TO CONSIDER | EXAMPLE |
|---------|-------------|---------|
| **Physical evidence** | Customer experience can change. Stores were geared up for in-store service where packaging, etc was controlled. | Glasses Direct only operates online and offers free samples of glasses in a specially-designed postal box, all ordered from its website. |
| **Processes** | Adapting the business to adopt online marketing. | MentionMe is a new online referral scheme that appears after a purchase is made, encouraging the user to recommend a friend. |

**See also**

Q77   How do we measure a digital campaign?
Q78   How do we monitor a digital campaign?
Q97   What best practice should we apply to our website and social channels?

## Q94     How do we develop our editorial calendar?

Your editorial calendar shows the strategic plans for your content for the year ahead.

Developing your editorial calendar in advance ensures that you have a clear content plan for the year. Create it in a spreadsheet and share with your team *via* Google Docs.

| | | EXISTING CUSTOMERS | | | NEW CUSTOMERS | | |
|---|---|---|---|---|---|---|---|
| MONTH | OUR EVENTS | BLOG | EMAIL | SOCIAL | BLOG | EMAIL | SOCIAL |
| JAN | | | | | | | |
| FEB | | | | | | | |
| MAR | | | | | | | |
| APR | | | | | | | |
| MAY | | | | | | | |
| JUN | | | | | | | |
| JUL | | | | | | | |
| AUG | | | | | | | |
| SEP | | | | | | | |
| OCT | | | | | | | |
| NOV | | | | | | | |
| DEC | | | | | | | |

Add in your key events, activities or planned promotions. Think about the time of year and what's relevant to your customer groups. You may sub-divide by quarter or month, depending on your business type.

The editorial calendar gives you a framework to get started and ensures you have a steady stream of content throughout the year. It means big events aren't missed and it enables you to plan ahead so, when you're busy, the work can be prepared in advance and scheduled, or shared with others. You can continue to add content in your normal way.

**See also**

## Q95    Which management tools save time?

The following tools will help you to save time in your social media marketing:

| TOOL | HOW IT SAVES TIME |
|------|-------------------|
| **Buffer** | Another free tool allows you to connect one social profile (for example, one Twitter, one Facebook, one LinkedIn account) and share the same message. You can schedule regular times for specific days when your messages appear or opt for a specific time and day. Files, images and documents can be added. |
| **Hootsuite** | This free tool allows you to connect up to five networks (for example, Facebook profile, Facebook Page, Twitter, LinkedIn, Google+) and share the same message across these channels. Messages can be scheduled to appear in the future. Files, images and documents can be added. You can monitor mentions of your company. |

Tweetdeck used to allow you to connect all social channels. Now owned by Twitter, it only allows you to manage Twitter.

These free tools have paid-for options that provide greater functionality.

**See also**
**Q56**    How can marketing automation make my life easier?

## Q96  How do we add admins to our social media channels?

Some channels enable you to add admins within the tool; others require a third party app to access the tool.

| SOCIAL CHANNEL | ADDING ADMINS |
| --- | --- |
| Blogs | In Blogger and WordPress, you can add new users easily and assign a role such as admin, content creator, etc. |
| Facebook | Anyone who has liked your page can become an admin. Facebook has different categories of admins from manager, content creator, moderator, advertiser and insights analyst. |
| Google+ | In your Google+ page, select 'Managers' and 'Add Manager'. There are two types of admins: owners and managers. A page can have only one owner, but can have up to 50 managers. |
| LinkedIn | Company page admins can be added as long as you are connected to the person. Go into your page, edit and scroll to Company Pages Admins and add people. |
| Slideshare | This channel is only available *via* one user name and password. Even the PRO version doesn't include multiple user access. |
| Twitter | At the moment, you can only manage Twitter through apps such as Hootsuite, Tweetdeck and Buffer. Alternatively, you share the user name and password with your admins – this is not great practice. |
| YouTube | As YouTube is owned by Google, you need to connect your YouTube channel to your Google+ page. Only the owner of the Google+ page can add or remove managers. Sign into the page owner's Google Account, select YouTube and in the channel's account settings select 'Add Managers' or 'Remove Managers'. |

**See also**
Q3   What are the key social marketing channels for B2C?
Q4   What are the key social marketing channels for B2B?

## Q97    What best practice should we apply to our website and social channels?

Regardless of channel, best practice is delivering what the customer wants and making it easy to access.

| BEST PRACTICE | HOW TO APPLY |
| --- | --- |
| **Use adaptive design** | This means it responds to the user, whether they're using a desktop PC, tablet or mobile phone of any type. It also means it delivers the relevant pages as fast as possible. |
| **Explain the rules of engagement** | If you provide customer service *via* your Facebook page, make sure you spell out on which days and times. If you don't provide customer service *via* the social network, explain how to access customer care and provide a telephone number or email. |
| **Be consistent** | Use the same images across all your social platforms and website. This helps the user to understand they have reached the right place. |
| **Explain key issues** | If there is a delivery charge, explain this early on. Don't make the customer wait until they get to the checkout to discover how much this will cost. |
| **Respond to queries** | Decide how to respond to queries and ensure all staff are aware of the process. Don't ignore customers, as they will continue to discuss you until they are happy. |
| **Think about the first line** | It's usually the first line of the response that's seen, so any negative words should be included lower down in the response. A good response thanks the customer for making contact, says who you are and that you'll deal with it personally. |

See also
**Q98**    How do we create a social media policy?

## Q98    How do we create a social media policy?

Most businesses have formal agreements in place with staff, often called 'Terms and Conditions of Employment'. This agreement usually states that the employee will not bring the company into disrepute and disclose company confidential information. In theory, this covers everything that would be in a social media policy. However, it may not be clear to all employees!

First, check to see whether you have a policy in place. If yes, ensure all your staff are aware of it. Perhaps mention in a staff meeting that clause 3.2 (or whichever) in the Terms and Conditions of Employment also covers use of all social media spaces.

If you are not covered, the Canadian website Social Media Policy Tool (**http://socialmedia.policytool.net**) provides a great starting point. It takes you through the major issues (mentioning the company outside work, speaking badly about customers, spending time at work updating your status) in plain English. As you move through the steps and answer the questions, the policy is created and at the end you simply copy and paste or request the document *via* email. When you have created the online policy, you can either adapt to your own business or seek advice from a legal expert to ensure your business is fully and legally covered.

**See also**
**Q16**    What legal issues can impact my business online?
**Q97**    What best practice should we apply to our website and social channels?

# Q99     Who should manage our social media?

Managing your social media is a question that needs to be considered. In the USA, the trend is to opt for outsourcing; in the UK and Ireland, this is seen as 'passing the buck'.

Whether you manage in-house or outsource depends on these factors:

- What are your objectives?
- Who is your target audience?
- How much time do you have?

B2C needs more management than B2B. So if you're in a B2C situation, you may wish to opt for a blended model of mainly in-house with some external support. If you're working within a well-known and larger brand, you are more likely to outsource many of the processes.

|  | B2B | B2C |
|---|:---:|:---:|
| **In-house** | ✓ | |
| **Some external support** | ✓ | ✓ |
| **Outsourced** | | ✓ |

Some external support could include one person spending an hour a week creating updates for you across your social channels. This may cost from €15 per hour depending on the skillset required. If you engage an agency to do this, expect to pay much more as their service will be enhanced and will include reporting. You can obtain external support from a range of websites, including PeoplePerHour and Elance. It's a good idea to prepare a brief specifying exactly what the freelancer can and can't do and to share all your policies with them.

**See also**
**Q95**    Which management tools save time?

# Q100    How do we engage an external agency?

To engage an external agency to manage or develop your social marketing, start by writing a clear brief, including information on:

- Where are you now? What's the background to this campaign, outsourcing, strategy?
- What do you want to achieve?
- Why now?
- What does success look like?
- Whose work do you admire, dislike and why?
- Who will 'own' the project?
- Why have you decided to outsource?
- What is the timescale – any specific dates?
- Who will be involved in the decision-making process?
- Has a budget been allocated and approved?
- Your market, whether it's geographically- or demographically-based.
- Your customers: Who you're targeting and where they are based.
- Your competitors: Who they are, what they're doing.
- Your suppliers (if essential as part of the distribution mechanism).
- Any tools used right now (Hootsuite, Buffer, Twitter, Facebook).

When you have prepared the brief, you can select an agency by speaking to colleagues, checking people out on LinkedIn, identifying people listed with accredited and professional bodies.

When you meet the agency, these are the key questions to ask:

- How can they make a difference?
- Who will be doing our work on a day-to-day basis?
- Who will be our account manager?
- How do the fees work?

- What's the actual process for (the service you need)?
- What's their greatest success?
- And their greatest failure? And why?
- How do they measure results?
- How is the work integrated with all other marketing activities?

To ensure the relationship is productive, don't abdicate once the agency has been appointed! They need a constant point of contact too and will expect you to respond quickly when information is needed.

**See also**

**Q63** What questions should we ask an agency when building a mobile app?

# ABOUT THE AUTHOR

**ANNMARIE HANLON** is a trainer and consultant in digital marketing strategy and business development of social media.

Her digital journey started in 1999, when she worked in 'internet marketing': creating wire frames and writing content for websites and blogs, identifying practical methods to engage and retain web visitors, and more recently taking traditional businesses into the social media environment. Annmarie has worked on consultancy projects in the UK, Ireland, Hong Kong and Italy, with clients from sectors including luxury brands, professional services, software, communications, health, leisure and media.

A keynote speaker on Digital Marketing for business organisations, a trainer with Emarketeers and a Visiting Lecturer at the University of Derby, Annmarie is a Fellow of the Chartered Institute of Marketing, a Member of the Marketing Institute Ireland and a Liveryman of the Worshipful Company of Marketors. She is the author of **Quick Win Marketing** and co-author of **Quick Win Digital Marketing** and is currently studying for a PhD investigating social media frameworks. You can follow her on Twitter @annmariehanlon and connect *via* LinkedIn.

# ABOUT THE QUICK WIN SERIES

The **QUICK WIN** series of books, ebooks and apps is designed for the modern, busy reader, who wants to learn enough to complete the immediate task at hand, but needs to see the information in context.

Topics published to date (in print, ebook and app formats) include:

- QUICK WIN B2B SALES.
- QUICK WIN BUSINESS COMMUNICATIONS.
- QUICK WIN DIGITAL MARKETING.
- QUICK WIN ECONOMICS.
- QUICK WIN HR IRELAND.
- QUICK WIN LEADERSHIP.
- QUICK WIN MARKETING.
- QUICK WIN MEDIA LAW IRELAND.
- QUICK WIN PRESENTATIONS.
- QUICK WIN PUBLIC RELATIONS.
- QUICK WIN SAFETY MANAGEMENT.
- QUICK WIN SOCIAL MEDIA MARKETING.

See **www.oaktreepress.com** / **www.SuccessStore.com**.

Lightning Source UK Ltd.
Milton Keynes UK
UKOW04f0245170114

224736UK00001B/9/P